Seder Interrupted: A Post-October 7 Hagaddah Supplement

Edited by Dr. Ora Horn Prouser
and Rabbi Menachem Creditor

Seder Interrupted: A Post-October 7 Hagaddah Supplement
First Printing
© 2024 by Menachem Creditor and Ora Horn Prouser
Cover © 2024 by Av Rimon + Studio Shoshan

ISBN: PP/ 9798884144408

I am at the Seder,
but my heart is in October.

Centuries ago, the Spanish Jewish poet Yehuda Halevi expressed both his sense of distance from, and connection to, the land of his ancestors: "לִבִּי בְמִזְרָח וְאָנֹכִי בְּסוֹף מַעֲרָב - My heart is in the East, and I am in the furthermost West." Many of us feel similarly today, in terms of both space and time. Months have passed, but for many Jews around the world, the traumatic events of October 7 feel ever present -- and in Israel this sense is even more acute. Many of us in the Diaspora feel the emotional connection to Israel, as well as the physical distance, as much as ever. We are here, but our hearts are there. And we are at the seder, but our hearts are still in שבעה באוקטובר *shiv'ah be-October* -- which can mean both "the 7th of October" and "the shiva [mourning period] of October."

3

Seder Interrupted:
A Post-October 7 Hagaddah
Supplement

CONTENTS

מצה / Matzah

מרור / Maror

שְׁפֹךְ חֲמָתְךָ / Pour Out Your Wrath

הלל / Hallel

נרצה / Nirtzah

ספירת העמר / Counting the Omer

שירים / *Songs and Poems*

Introduction

As we prepare to celebrate Passover, we find ourselves in uncharted territory. We celebrate freedom during Passover, but what is the definition of freedom this year? As we are still reeling from the horrors of October 7, and the ensuing events both in Israel and in the United States, as we are still praying and working for the release of our hostages, we are left with many questions, and not many answers. That does feel particularly appropriate to Passover, as the asking of questions is central to the Seder. These questions, however, are far more difficult and filled with pain and fear. These questions leave us wondering how to engage with Passover this year.

How are we thinking about the definition of freedom this year? How do we read *Vehi She'amdah* as we see on a daily basis those who "seek our destruction"? What is the meaning *in L'shanah Haba'ah B'yerushalayim* as many in the American Jewish community are strengthening connections to Israel and while there are many who are struggling with Israel's response? What will we be thinking during *Shefokh Hamatkha* with its call for God's anger against our enemies? And how do we deal with our own anger, rage, fear, terror, and deep pain?

The creation of this supplement to the Pesach Haggadah is especially fitting for the Academy for Jewish Religion as it is a product of our core values. At AJR we believe in the relevance of traditional sacred literature and our responsibility to connect it to our own times. At AJR we believe that each person has the right and responsibility to find their place in Jewish thought and tradition, and that we do well when we reach out to others where they are. At AJR we cherish diversity and a variety of approaches to Jewish life. We know that we each become stronger and deeper in our own understandings when we engage with and learn from those with whom we disagree. At the same time, we believe that each pluralistic community needs to determine its borders and to determine what lies within its pluralism.

We have engaged with this project as an expression of our belief in Zionism, and in solidarity with Israel and the Jewish People. We recognize that Zionism can be a large tent, but that there are views that fall outside of the Zionist tent, and that are outside of AJR's pluralism. While this path may seem difficult to navigate, those of us at AJR have been trained to embrace these types of struggles and difficulties. And we have learned to do it with patience, caring, and love.

We want to thank all those who have made this project possible. Thank you to AJR rabbinical student Pam Ehrenkranz, who engaged in early conversations that led to this project. Thank you to Rabbi Menachem Creditor who put so much time, effort, care, and a deep sense of mission into this book. Thank you to those on the AJR administration and staff who stepped in when we needed help of all kinds. Thank you to all of our contributors, who shared their thoughts, fears, and hopes with us in their writing and artwork.

We hope that you find this supplement helpful as you prepare for your Seder this year. You will find in it pieces that are comforting. You may also find material that makes you uncomfortable. You will find selections that express your own thoughts, and those with which you may disagree. We mostly hope, however, that you find support and connection in the knowledge that others are struggling just as you are, and that working together, we can start to engage with these important questions, even if we are not yet able to find all the answers.

לשנה הבאה בירושלים הבנויה
Next year in Jerusalem – in peace.

Dr. Ora Horn Prouser
CEO and Academic Dean,
Academy for Jewish Religion
Adar II, 2024

Order

Rabbi Beth Naditch

In the days and weeks after October 7th, chaos swirled. Safety, meaning, and narrative were shredded on that day, and in the ensuing time as the drums of anti-Semitic tropes grow louder, it has been hard to find secure footing in the world. The answer to the simple question of "How are you?" has moved from polite platitude to impossible and intractable puzzle. I found, in those early weeks, that my only possible answer to that question was "Shattered." As our ancestors carried the smashed tablets of the covenant alongside the whole ones as we traveled through the wilderness, I hoped that our community had an ark strong enough to hold the sharp slivers, the rough pieces, the broken fragments of everything that has splintered.

For me, an early moment of respite arose when I found my way to an expressive arts therapist who threw open her studio to people impacted. Around tables with art supplies, our community of disparate mourners gathered. We had never met before but shared a connection to Israel and to the Jewish people. Some had lost relatives in the massacre, some had family and friends under regular rocket attack, others cherished their own connections, experiences, and the place of Israel

15

in their lives. While I, as a rabbi and chaplain, use tools of words and a listening ear as ways of responding to suffering, the expressive artist could pick up where words felt limiting or were elusive. She offered the tools and materials of creating art as a way to contain, or at least express, the swirling chaos. From her I learned that working with a round canvas, much like the seder plates on our tables tonight, can be healing. That first session, our medium was colored glass. My hands and heart seemed to know the order they craved as they pulled together colors and pieces into a mosaic on a small, round, board - the shattered pieces ultimately forming a coherent whole.

Two thousand years earlier, in the wake of the destruction of the Temple and tremendous unrest, the rabbis used all the creative tools in their hands to restore order out of the chaos of destruction. Our seder, whose very name means order, offers us now familiar ritual so that we can step out of times of shattering chaos, even momentarily. It helps us to bring those fragments into an organized and coherent whole. Modern trauma theory eventually recognized what the rabbis knew instinctively: Where trauma overwhelms, provide sensory grounding and order.

Kadesh, Urchatz, Karpas, Yachatz, we recite, as we bring our senses into the present: the taste of the wine, the feel of the water on our hands, the smell of the parsley, the sound of the breaking matzah, the sight of the symbols of the holiday we have been observing since that night of tumult as we fled from Egypt.

Maggid, Rachtzah, Motzi Matzah, we sing, as we painstakingly tell the story of pain and redemption, slavery and freedom, taking what feels shattered and reassembling into a clear picture that restores narrative coherence.

Maror Korech Shulchan Orech: Some years, we relate better to the sweetness of the charoset, but in others, it feels integrating to match the maelstrom inside with the bitterness of the maror. We eat, recognizing that even when the world doesn't make sense, we need to endure.

Tzafun Barekh Hallel Nirtzah: the meaning and solutions seem hidden now, and in response we engage in a practice of gratitude for what might have at this moment. There is comfort in familiar liturgy and songs, traditions that tie us to less fraught times and evoke connections to family. As we call out from the narrow place, we pray that while today we might be shattered, perhaps next year we will have some comfort of coherence again.

Rabbi Beth Naditch is an ACPE Certified Educator/Rabbi at Hebrew Senior Life in Massachusetts.

יחץ
Yachatz

Division and Uncertainty in our Moments of Crisis

Rabbi Matthew Goldstone PhD

The seder is full of "fours" – the four cups, the four questions, the four children, etc. But there is another, relatively unknown, four in the Passover story from when the Israelites were standing before the sea and Pharaoh's army was approaching. According to the midrash:

> "The Israelites at the Red Sea were divided into four groups. One group said: Let us throw ourselves into the sea. One said: Let us return to Egypt. One said: Let us fight them; and one said: Let us cry out against them."[1]

At the moment of crisis, when they were ostensibly trapped between sword and water, the people could not agree on the proper course of action.

At our seders this year we might find divisions among family and friends as to what should have been done in response to the events of October 7th and what Israel – and the world Jewish community – should do next. Or we ourselves, as individuals, might be internally conflicted about decisions – big

---

[1] Mechilta deRabbi Ishmael Beshallach Parashah 2; H. S Horovitz and I. A. Rabin, *Mechilta D'Rabbi Ismael cum variis lectionibus et adnotationibus* (Jerusalem: Bamberger & Wahrmann, 1970), 96; J. Z. Lauterbach, *Mekhilta De-Rabbi Ishmael a Critical Edition, Based on the Manuscripts and Early Editions*, vol. 1 (Philadelphia, PA: Jewish Publication Society, 2004), 214. Note: Some versions of this tradition (such as the one in *Pirkei deRabbeinu HaKodesh*) only describe three groups of Israelites.

or small – that Israel and our communities have made in response to the act of terror and ensuing antisemitism.

Like the ancient Israelites, Jews today hold different opinions about the best course of action in moments of crisis. Ultimately, in the Exodus story, it turns out that none of the Israelites' recommended responses carried the day. Instead, Moses pleaded that the people trust in God, and God intervened to provide redemption. While we cannot simply wait for miraculous intervention today, the midrash teaches us that we do not need to have all of the right answers, and sometimes, in moments of crisis, we simply do not know the correct path to take.

The midrash[2] also records another tradition about the Israelites arguing at the shore of the sea.[3] However, we have conflicting manuscript evidence for this midrash.

According to one version:

> "When the Israelites stood at the sea, one said: 'I will go down to the sea first' and the other said: 'I will go down to the sea first.'"

According to another version of the tradition:

> "When the Israelites stood at the sea, one said: 'I will not go down to the sea first' and the other said: 'I will not go down to the sea first.'"

---

[2] Mechilta deRabbi Ishmael Beshallah Parashah 5
[3] Horovitz and Rabin, 106; Lauterbach, 1:234 (my translation here deviates from Lauterbach).

The visual difference between these two possibilities is a simple letter *yud* – the difference between אני and איני.[4] The coexistence of these versions of the midrashic tradition can resonate with our experience. At times like this we may feel compelled to act immediately and yet be paralyzed by fear or indecision, or we may do everything that we can think of and yet still feel that it is inadequate. Or, like the disagreement of the previous midrash, we may be so conflicted individually or among ourselves as to the correct course of action that we end up caught in the space between the אני and the איני, between certainty and hesitancy.[5]

At our seders this year, let us remember that disagreement and uncertainty are inherent in the Exodus experience but that even with their conflicts the Israelites emerged from the sea as one nation. And like our ancestors, let us hope that we may also merit the sheltering presence of the divine to protect us in our moments of uncertainty and danger.

Rabbi Matthew Goldstone, PhD is the Assistant Academic Dean and Assistant Professor of Talmud and Rabbinics at the Academy for Jewish Religion.

---

[4] According to some, there might not even be a letter difference since the word איני ("I will not") can also be written without the extra yud, making it appear exactly like the word אני ("I").

[5] For more on the two aforementioned midrashim, and for the inspiration behind this piece, see the analysis in Hebrew in M. Kister, *Dynamics of Midrashic Traditions in Second Temple and Rabbinic Literature* (Jerusalem: Magnes Press, 2024): 298-311.

מַגִּיד
Maggid

Ha Lachma Anya:
A Poem

Dr. Rachel Posner

Every year I am more me,
and every year
matzah tastes more
like loosening a tie,
kicking off my shoes:
like home

"All who are hungry" means more every year
and every year I am hungrier,
softer, angrier

Every year these words grow to contain
my hunger, my softness, my rage
Every year I find more matzah,
more life pounding in my chest
more sparks, more breath,
more Torah to taste and to share

So we set out on our journey again -
We do not even need to pack:
Everything we own already stuffed
in a backpack, waiting at the door

Every year you are more you:
distilled and clear; flowing light
So the table expands and the flames
reach higher and the light travels out, out
past the house where Elijah stops for the night,
weary, hollow, pulsing with hope…
He holds his feverish joy aloft for all to see:
this is the bread of affliction.

Dr. Rachel Posner is a rabbinical student at the
Academy for Jewish Religion and a practicing
psychologist.

A Night for Serious Questions

Dr. David Arnow

> Know well that your ancestors shall be strangers in a land not theirs, and they shall be enslaved and oppressed for four hundred years… and in the end they shall go forth with great wealth.
>
> —Haggadah, quoting Genesis 15:13-14

God speaks these words to Abraham and the Haggadah cites them to argue that the story of the Exodus didn't just happen. It was destined to occur. And the story's contours will model the ceaseless ebb and flow of Jewish history: "from slavery to freedom, from grief to joy, from mourning to festivity, from darkness to great light, and from subjugation to redemption" as the Haggadah puts it.

Like most Jewish liturgy, the Haggadah emphasizes praising God for our redemption rather than probing the causes of our suffering — in this case centuries of enslavement. This may create the misimpression that rabbinic thought shies away from the matter. Over the ages our sources have offered many reasons for the bondage in Egypt. Here's a very small sample:

1) Rav said: "A parent should never give one child preferential treatment over others. It was because of one ounce of fine wool that Jacob gave to Joseph … when making him the striped coat that his brothers became jealous of him. And that led to our ancestors going down to Egypt."[6]

2) God said to the sons of Jacob: "You sold Joseph for a slave… By your lives, year after year you will be reciting *We were slaves of Pharaoh in Egypt," avadim hayinu l'Pharaoh*.[7]

3) In the process of selling grain during the famine, Joseph acquired all the Egyptians' money, livestock, and land for Pharaoh. "And he removed the population town by town, from one end of Egypt's border to the other."[8] Joseph then gave them seed to plant and in return required a fifth of their annual harvest for Pharaoh. "And they said to him, 'You have saved our lives! …We will be slaves to Pharaoh (*v'hayinu avadim l'Pharaoh*). "A generation later, the Egyptians would take their revenge on Joseph for having reduced them to slavery, by enslaving his people."[9]

---

[6] Babylonian Talmud Shabbat 10b
[7] Midrash on Psalms 10:3
[8] Gen. 47:21
[9] *Etz Hayim: Torah and Commentary*, Rabbinical Assembly, 2001, p. 288

If you take God out of the equation, these texts suggest that particular failings of Jacob, Joseph, and his brothers set in motion a chain of events that ended in disaster for their descendants. Without absolving Pharaoh of his genocidal cruelty, they warn us that our own actions may have unintended consequences that contribute to our reversals of fortune. That lesson is never easy to accept. But it points the way to facing the present with a stronger sense of agency and the future with a deeper capacity to choose hope over despair.

Questions for discussion:

1) *In what ways does this Passover feel different than other Passovers?*
2) *Does the point of view reflected in the texts cited above add to your understanding of the Passover story? If so, how?*
3) *Given legitimate concerns about blaming the victim, what are the strengths and weaknesses of this approach?*
4) *Texts like these ask us to look inward and to assume a measure of responsibility for the situations in which we find ourselves as individuals and as a people. In our post-October 7th world what would that entail?*

David Arnow, PhD is the author of *Creating Lively Passover Seders* and co-editor of *My People's Passover Haggadah*. His most recent book is *Choosing Hope: The Heritage of Judaism.*

Enslavement and Salvation

Rabbi Eliezer Diamond, PhD

The Exodus story is told in two different ways in the Haggadah. The first is in the *Avadim Hayinu*, "We Were Slaves", section at the beginning of Maggid. It speaks of the Exodus as an event in the distant past and it acknowledges that those sitting at the seder table and enjoying the fruits of freedom might have a difficult time seeing the relevance of that story to their lives. Therefore, the Haggadah reminds us that no matter how distant we are chronologically from the exodus from Egypt, our present-day freedom is possible only because of God's redemption of our ancestors long ago. Had that salvational act not occured, "we, our children, and our children's children would all be slaves to Pharoah." It would be a different Pharaoh, but in the end, they are all the same.

There is a second version of the story, and it is directed toward a different audience, one that has experienced or is experiencing oppression. Quoting from Joshua's farewell speech, the Haggadah reminds us that in the beginning we were enslaved not in body but in that we were bound to idolatry. We bowed to false gods and worshipped them. Joshua/the Haggadah then tells us how our ancestors turned away from idolatry and toward the one true God. The story of the Patriarchs is then recounted in brief form: Abraham emigrates to Canaan and has a son, Yitzhak. He in turn has two sons, Esau and Jacob. Although Joshua recounts all of Israelite history until his own day, the Haggadah's citation of Joshua's words ends with the following words:

> "And I [=God] granted Esau Mount Seir and Jacob and his sons went down to Egypt."[10]

To end the citation of Joshua's speech at this point is curious. Joshua goes on to describe the redemption from Egypt, which is after all what we are celebrating. Why not include those words?

It seems that the Haggadah is acknowledging and wrestling with a troubling fact that was ignored in the first telling. True, God brought us up from Egypt, but it was also God who brought us there, not least by encouraging Jacob to go to Egypt. Why would God do this? Would it not have been a much greater kindness to spare us from slavery altogether?

The Haggadah offers an impenetrable answer to these questions. As part of its response, it conveys a promise that is simultaneously troubling and consoling: "*In every generation they have risen up to exterminate us.*" The enslavement

---

[10] Joshua 24:4

in Egypt was not a one-time event; it was meant to serve as an archetype for all of Jewish history. Indeed, we have experienced many Egypts, many oppressors, and the Haggadah implies that we will experience more. The promise is only that each time "God saves us from their hands."

What does this mean? So often the salvation has come only after many have been tortured and killed. The only way we can understand this is that the promise is not that any one individual is promised salvation but rather the nation as a whole.

As Jews, each of us needs to decide whether to accept the at times unbearable fate that has been decreed for us. Does a catastrophe, such as the one that took place on October 7th, convince us to give up now rather than wait for some future salvation? The Haggadah is urging us to hang on. To be part of the Jewish people is to learn to keep the faith even in the worst moments, not just for one's own sake but for the sake of the people of Israel. We must live through this difficult time even though we cannot see salvation on the horizon. We can only hope that through God's help and our own efforts, we will move "*from darkness to light, from enslavement to redemption.*" May it be so.

Rabbi Eliezer Diamond, PhD is the Rabbi Judah Nadich Professor of Talmud and Rabbinics at the Jewish Theological Seminary.

עבדים היינו
Avadim Hayinu
We Were Enslaved

Ilu – אִלּוּ

Rabbi David Greenstein, PhD

The word "*ilu*" is the pivotal word of the Haggadah, the Passover storytelling. This tiny Hebrew word combines two words – *im* - אם- and *lu* – לוּ. The first word – *im* - means "if". It is a word that points to the future and to open-ended possibilities and opportunities – and hope. The second word – *lu* – means "if only" or "would it have been the case" and points backward to lost chances, regrets and dreads. In the word, *ilu*, we bring together these opposing perspectives, sensing both possibilities and impossibilities.

The word first appears in the middle of our response to the beloved introduction of the Haggadah, the Four Questions. We rightly celebrate the first sentence of that answer:

> "We were slaves to Pharaoh in Egypt and the Eternal, our Almighty God, took us out with a mighty Hand and an outstretched Arm!"

And we embrace the end of the paragraph that encourages us to increase our engagement in the Telling. But we too often ignore the middle of the paragraph, the sentence that begins with *ilu*:

> "But if – *ilu* - the Holy Blessed One *had not* taken us out of Egypt, then we and our children and our children's children would still be enslaved to Pharaoh in Egypt."

What an extraordinary claim! It tells us that had the Exodus not happened when it did, it would *never* have happened, *ever*, and even today, thousands of years later, our own view of the future would be overwhelmed with the hopelessness of slavery. We would *know* that our own grandchildren would surely eternally be slaves. The implications are dark. There are at least two to start with: We should understand that, without God's intervention at a very specific moment in history, God would not have intervened ever again. And we would never become free by any other means, for, without that Divine effort, no amount of human effort would ever be able to make a difference.

Do we ignore this sentence because it is so profoundly unsettling and challenging?

Yet this statement is crucial to our Story because of the third implication that follows from it. The terror of perpetual enslavement and the abandonment of all hope is countered by the fact that God *did* take us out of Egypt at that specific, unique and last moment! And so, we delight in our freedom and good fortune. But we are called to celebrate with a new consciousness, an "*ilu* consciousness." Our "*ilu* consciousness" calls us to realize that God's effort has made possible our hope in our own efforts. Thanks to God's mighty Hand and outstretched Arm our own hands and arms, ears, and hearts are freed to feel, to hear, to act. "*Ilu* consciousness" has us remember our pain and terror and despair along with looking forward to singing "a *new* song." So we conclude this section of the Telling with a glorious litany of *ilu* declarations – the beloved poem *Dayenu*. "*Ilu* consciousness" demands that we remember the powerlessness and despair of our past precisely at the same time that we are released into history, into the opportunity and the challenge to address the real possibilities that we can achieve – though these may be only incomplete states of redemption. We are free to hope realistically.

"*Ilu* consciousness" tells us that the unique moment of Divine liberation happened only once in mundane history. Now it is we who must respond to the unique demands of our own time, a time of incomparable crisis.

How shall we respond? If we are meant to know the harsh feelings of oppression and despair even in the midst of our liberation, surely it is so that we will not keep repeating our refusal to pursue every avenue that will free us from oppressing others and denying them their freedom. As we spill out drops of wine to mourn for our ancient foes, so, surely, must we feel the tragedy of our present foes and neighbors. If we do not do this, then what does our ceremony mean for us? As the Haggadah says – "*Ilu* – had we been in Egypt with that mindset – we would not have been redeemed."

Rabbi David Greenstein, PhD is a retired rabbi who is currently a teacher at seminaries and institutions of higher learning and an artist. He is an alumnus and past President and Rosh HaYeshiva at the Academy for Jewish Religion.

To Make a Short Story Long

Shalom Orzach

For THE companion for great storytelling, the Haggadah sometimes overly uses the technique of keeping us in suspense. The *Ma'aseh*, the tale occurs in Bnei Brak, you will remember it well;

מַעֲשֶׂה בְּרַבִּי אֱלִיעֶזֶר וְרַבִּי יְהוֹשֻׁעַ וְרַבִּי אֶלְעָזָר בֶּן־
עֲזַרְיָה וְרַבִּי עֲקִיבָא וְרַבִּי טַרְפוֹן שֶׁהָיוּ מְסֻבִּין בִּבְנֵי־בְרַק
וְהָיוּ מְסַפְּרִים בִּיצִיאַת מִצְרַיִם כָּל־אוֹתוֹ הַלַּיְלָה, עַד
שֶׁבָּאוּ תַלְמִידֵיהֶם וְאָמְרוּ לָהֶם רַבּוֹתֵינוּ הִגִּיעַ זְמַן
קְרִיאַת שְׁמַע שֶׁל שַׁחֲרִית.

It happened once [on Pesach] that Rabbi Eliezer, Rabbi Yehoshua, Rabbi Elazar ben Azariah, Rabbi Akiva and Rabbi Tarfon were reclining in Bnei Brak and were telling the story of the exodus from Egypt that whole night, until their students came and said to them, "The time of reciting the morning Shema has arrived."

With these giants of their generation, why not share the stories of the exodus they actually told? The insights, elucidations, and implications for how we are to live must surely have been remarkable, and yet in this rare invitation to almost join these prestigious scholars, the *chidushim,* the novel and innovation interpretations are conspicuously missing.

Some will suggest that the context becomes a proof text for the directive closing the previous paragraph:

וְכָל הַמַּרְבֶּה לְסַפֵּר בִּיצִיאַת מִצְרַיִם הֲרֵי זֶה מְשֻׁבָּח

> And those who add and spend extra time in telling the story of the exodus from Egypt, behold they are surely praiseworthy.

Yes and… why not provide these details too? Their additions must be worthy of learning if not reciting as well!

I wish to suggest that there is an additional charge that informs this approach, that of "in each generation…" We must craft our own stories pertinent to our particular circumstances in our generation. Stories and callings for our time. How do the challenges as well as the opportunities and the anguish of our reality invite the timely yet timeless stories we must tell? This year the onus is all the more acute.

I believe there is more, in the silence, we hear the angst. How is it possible to elaborate on experiences that are so traumatic? Might we suggest that this was the content if not the dilemma that kept them up all night; What can we say? What can we teach? What can we learn? It is the audacity and bravery to enter that "Pardes", that conundrum, that is being praised if not encouraged. Our ability to heal arises out of our ability to relate and share these experiences with supportive and compassionate friends and family. The *sippur yetziat Mitzrayim*, the accounts of our pleas to be released from the confines, from the deep tunnels, from the horror suffered, will require unrivaled bravery and the tenacity to hope for and believe in better days that will revive our ability להיות עם חופשי בארצנו - To be a Free People in our Land…

Curiously the closing of the story does contain details, whilst the teachers are silent, the pupils are given voice. This in and of itself is worthy of telling! The Talmid is the Chacham, the pupil becomes the teacher. It is astounding and this year we too must listen hard to all the voices, particularly to those that may not be heard. It is our pupils, our children that will remind us that a new dawn has begun, we have much to do, but in our *na'aseh* our doing, we must not neglect our *nishma,* our obligation to hear. - הִגִּיעַ זְמַן קְרִיאַת שְׁמַע the time has come, the calling to hear! We must diligently collect and tell the stories, to honor the memories of the fallen, to share their legacies and become their voices. The countless stories of bravery, of showing up, of the inspirational volunteerism must also be told.

וְכָל הַמַּרְבֶּה... הֲרֵי זֶה מְשֻׁבָּח

And all who meticulously elaborate, behold they are surely praiseworthy.

Shalom Orzach is a senior educator and consultant for The iCenter for Israel Education.

The Four Sins[11]

Rabbi Joseph H. Prouser

אָנָּא יְיָ הוֹשִׁיעָה נָּא.

"Please, God, deliver us!"

כֹּה אָמַר יְיָ עַל־שְׁלֹשָׁה פִּשְׁעֵי עַזָּה וְעַל־אַרְבָּעָה לֹא אֲשִׁיבֶנּוּ
עַל־הַגְלוֹתָם גָּלוּת שְׁלֵמָה לְהַסְגִּיר לֶאֱדוֹם :

"Thus said God:
'For three sins of Gaza, for four, I will not turn
away from punishment: because they took
many hostages into captivity, whom they
delivered to Edom."

כְּנֶגֶד אַרְבָּעָה חֲטוּפִים דִּבְּרָה תוֹרָה. כַּכָּתוּב :
אֶת־כָּל־הַיְּהוּדִים מִנַּעַר וְעַד־זָקֵן טַף וְנָשִׁים בְּיוֹם אֶחָד.

Our Torah speaks of four categories of
hostages, as it is written: "All the Jews, young
men and elders, infants and women, on a
single day..."

---

[11] *Sources cited:* The opening and closing phrases are taken from
the Simchat Torah liturgy. *Introduction:* Psalm 118:25; Amos 1:6;
Esther 3:13. *The Elders:* Leviticus 19:32; Kiddushin 32b;
Lamentations 5:12; Genesis 6:13. *The Women:* Proverbs 13:2;
Lamentations 5:3, 11; Exodus 23:1. *The Young Men:* Obadiah 1:10;
Genesis 25:27. *The Infants:* Isaiah 60:18; 2 Samuel 12:22.

זָקֵן מַה הוּא אוֹמֵר?
מָה הָעֵדֹת וְהַחֻקִּים וְהַמִּשְׁפָּטִים,
אֲשֶׁר צִוָּה יְיָ אֱלֹהֵינוּ אֶתְכֶם?
וְאַף אַתָּה אֱמָר־לוֹ:
וְהָדַרְתָּ פְּנֵי זָקֵן, וְאֵין זָקֵן אֶלָּא

חָכָם.

שָׂרִים בְּיָדָם נִתְלוּ פְּנֵי זְקֵנִים לֹא נֶהְדָּרוּ,
כִּי־מָלְאָה הָאָרֶץ חָמָס מִפְּנֵיהֶם.

What do the elders say? "What are the
laws, regulations, and statutes
which the Lord our God commanded
you?"
Answer them, saying: "Show deference
to the aged." And "aged" can mean
only

The Wise.

"They hanged princes with their own
hands, they showed no deference to
elders."
"For the land was filled with Hamas -
violence, lawlessness, moral anarchy -
because of them."

נָשִׁים מַה הֵן אוֹמְרוֹת ? וְנֶפֶשׁ בֹּגְדִים
חָמָס, אִמֹּתֵינוּ כְּאַלְמָנוֹת,
נָשִׁים בְּצִיּוֹן עֻנּוּ,אַל־תָּשֶׁת יָדְךָ עִם

רָשָׁע

לִהְיֹת עֵד חָמָס. אִלּוּ הָיִיתָ שָׁם,
לֹא הָיִיתָ נִגְאָל :

What do the women say? "The
appetite, the desire of the degenerate is
for Hamas - violence, lawlessness,
moral anarchy"-
"Our mothers are widowed; women
have been raped in Zion;"
"Give no quarter to

The Wicked

who perpetrate Hamas - violence,
lawlessness, moral anarchy."
Had you been there, you would not
have been spared.

נַעַר מַה הוּא אוֹמֵר? מֵחֲמַס אָחִיךָ יַעֲקֹב
תְּכַסְּךָ בוּשָׁה וְנִכְרַתָּ לְעוֹלָם
וְיַעֲקֹב אִישׁ

תָּם

יֹשֵׁב אֹהָלִים.

What do the young men say? "For the
Hamas - the violence, lawlessness,
moral anarchy - visited upon your
brother Jacob, disgrace shall engulf
you and you shall perish forever." For
"Jacob was

A Man with the
Simplest of Desires:
to have peace and security in his
home."

וְטַף ? אֵתְ פְּתַח לוֹ. שֶׁנֶּאֱמַר:
לֹא־יִשָּׁמַע עוֹד חָמָס בְּאַרְצֵךְ,
אָמַרְתִּי

מִי יוֹדֵעַ

וְחַנַּנִי יְיָ וְחַי הַיָּלֶד.

And the infants? You must initiate the
conversation, saying: "No more shall
Hamas
- violence, lawlessness, moral anarchy -
be heard of in the Land."
"I say:

Who Knows?

Perhaps God will have mercy and my
child shall live."

אָנָּא יְיָ, עֲנֵנוּ בְיוֹם קָרְאֵנוּ.
Please, God, answer us
on the day we cry out to You!

Joseph H. Prouser is rabbi of Temple Emanuel of North
Jersey in Franklin Lakes, and editor of *Masorti: The New
Journal of Conservative Judaism*.

She who Rose Up to Stand for Us and for Humanity

Rabbi Dianne Cohler-Esses

וְהִיא שֶׁעָמְדָה לַאֲבוֹתֵינוּ וְלָנוּ. שֶׁלֹּא אֶחָד בִּלְבָד עָמַד
עָלֵינוּ לְכַלוֹתֵנוּ, אֶלָּא שֶׁבְּכָל דּוֹר וָדוֹר עוֹמְדִים עָלֵינוּ
לְכַלוֹתֵנוּ, וְהַקָּדוֹשׁ בָּרוּךְ הוּא מַצִּילֵנוּ מִיָּדָם.

And it is this that has stood for our ancestors and for us; since it is not only one that has stood against us to destroy us, but rather in each generation, they stand against us to destroy us, but the Holy Blessed One rescues us from their hand.

Vehi sheamda – And "She" that stood

I can feel her presence even now, even in this broken generation. She is standing at a distance, watching us, waiting for the moment to ripen, ready to step in.

Who is this mysterious "she" that stood for our ancestors and for us?

Traditionally "she" has been read as "The Torah" or "the *Shechinah*", God's feminine presence who dwells close to us always.

But I read it differently. For this broken moment my "she" is human, an ancestor. It is Miriam, Miriam the slave girl, Miriam the prophet.

Why Miriam? Because she stood. And in that standing "she" (!) ultimately saves an entire people.

She stood while her imperiled baby brother – who was so threatening to the Pharaoh that he wanted him dead –was placed by his heartbroken mother in a basket in the reeds by the River Nile.

וַתֵּתַצַּב אֲחֹתוֹ מֵרָחֹק לְדֵעָ֫ה מַה־יֵּעָשֶׂה לֽוֹ:

And she stood. Miriam watched him. She waited. She would not abandon him.

She waited for "*de'ah*" for revelation, for the moment when she was called to act.

And when was the right moment? When her enemy, her enslaver, the one who wanted her brother dead, the daughter of Pharaoh, came down to the Nile with her servant girls to bathe. To bathe!! As if all was right in her empire, as if Hebrew babies were not being drowned in the Nile. She went to bathe as if innocent blood was not drenching her land and flowing through the waters of the river where she bathes.

But Miriam knew better than to see her oppressor as simply an oppressor. As less than human. She expected humanity even from her enemy. Impossibly, she watched with eyes of hope.

47

Here's how the scene unfolds: The daughter of Pharaoh sees a basket, sends her servant girl to fetch it, and opens it. When she sees a baby crying, she opens her heart. Despite her father's terrible edict, she has compassion, she recognizes the humanity of the wailing Hebrew infant before her.

That is the moment Miriam has been waiting for. She steps in and dares to speak to the daughter of Pharaoh as a peer rather than a princess, as a human rather than a harsh oppressor. Miriam sees the signs of humanity in *Bat Pharaoh* - and asks for more.

She addresses her as a partner, as a co-conspirator: "*Shall I go and call a nursing woman from the Hebrews for you, that she may nurse the child for you?*"[12] she asks.

And with that she reunites child and mother, allowing her mother a few precious years to hold her precious son close, deferring grief until he is old enough to be taken to the palace to his adoptive mother, the daughter of Pharaoh.

וְהִיא שֶׁעָמְדָה לַאֲבוֹתֵינוּ וְלָנוּ

Miriam is the one who stands and watches, who waits in faith for that precise redemptive moment.

---

[12] Ex. 2:7

Miriam is the slave girl who makes deals for the sake of redemption.

Miriam is the one who recognizes the humanity of her oppressor, crossing enemy lines to save life.

I can sense her presence even now in this shattered moment. Miriam is waiting, watching for just the right moment to step in, into the human field, into the field of redemption, and save our people.

Dianne Cohler-Esses is the Rabbi and Director of Lifelong Learning at Romemu in New York City.

From the River to the Sea
Rabbi David Ehrenkranz

It split once for Moses and once for Joshua.
The water ran away from them
Like the fox in my backyard who
Runs away from my dog.

The fear is different
But the result is the same.
One runs and hides and the other
 Crosses without worry.

 I listen to the chants
For the water to split again
And then drown the people
Who purify water and cure illnesses.

The ones who yell are like the fox
Who thinks he is winning by killing my chickens,
Tearing up my garden and
Multiplying faster than I can see.

It seems they have all taken a toxic bath
Of hate and do not realize
That the waters are not going to split again,
 And my dog, who loves life, will soon end the hatred.

Rabbi David Ehrenkranz is an Upper School Judaic
Studies Teacher at Maimonides School in
Massachusetts.

Yad Labanim During Israel's Involvement in Lebanon

Danny Siegel

> Yad LaBanim is a memorial in Jerusalem for those who died defending the City, and citizens of Jerusalem wo defended Israel on all fronts, since the time the Turks ruled the country.

There's new names to put up now,
glistening in metal.
They're over the seven hundred mark,
but you can't read more than a few at a time
for the hurt.

There's three parts to this place, Tourists:
An office, modestly set.
A huge airy room with names
and more names
on the walls.
And a small room with shelves
and with files
with pictures
with stories
with letters
with articles and clippings
one for everyone who died.
Anything they could gather about the dead
they gathered
from the family
from the friends
from the newspapers

from anywhere they could gather.

The man from the modest office
showed us a file;
he shouldn't have done that.
Now they're no longer cardboard files.
Now they're no longer just names.

Danny Siegel is a poet, storyteller, and lecturer, who has been an important voice in discussions of Tzedakah and Tikkun Olam for many years. This previously published poem appears with the author's permission.

Anna Abramzon, "We Will Dance Again"

Let Me Count the Ways and the Plagues

Beth Steinberg

The Haggadah has many dramatic storytelling moments, one being the recitation of the ten plagues, a fearful list of afflictions and horrors witnessed and experienced by the Egyptians. The Children of Israel, while saved from the personal suffering caused by the plagues, had to have seen the hardship of the Egyptians, before miraculously exiting the scene for their 40-year sojourn in the desert. And what they missed in Goshen, because the plagues didn't happen there, they certainly saw firsthand during the crossing of the Red Sea, as the Egyptian Army chased them into the sea and drowned in front of them, in perhaps the final and most violent plague of them all.

Dramatic, but not so easy to take in and absorb.

How did the Children of Israel feel about the Egyptians' pain and suffering throughout the period of the plagues, starting with the bloodied Nile River, which had to be terrifying to everyone in Egypt? The plagues continued on to frogs and crop-destroying hail, culminating in fearful darkness so thick and scary that you couldn't see your hand, and the horrific deaths of first-born Egyptian children. Or, were they so astounded by God's wrath and power, a power with which they weren't that familiar during 400 years of slavery, that they were cowed and fearful, or vengeful and even angry over the calamitous events?

The ten plagues, and the long-term effects which they must have had, including crop and cattle collapse which surely must have led to financial instability for rank-and-file Egyptians, then followed by ill health from boils, vermin, and the death of the first-born children, always seemed like more than enough punishment for the Egyptian people.

During the reading of the Haggadah, the recitation of the plagues are accompanied by dipping one's finger into wine, one dip for each plague, a sort of ritual bloodletting to accompany the violence that the plagues begot. That retelling is followed by Rabbi Yehuda's acrostic, a seemingly playful but nonsensical way of remembering the plagues.

רַבִּי יְהוּדָה הָיָה נוֹתֵן בָּהֶם סִמָּנִים:
דְּצַ"ךְ עַדַ"שׁ בְּאַחַ"ב.

> "Rabbi Yehuda was accustomed to giving [the plagues] mnemonics: *Detzach* [the Hebrew initials of the first three plagues], *Adash* [the Hebrew initials of the second three plagues], *Be'achav* [the Hebrew initials of the last four plagues]."[13]

---

[13] Haggadah, Sefaria Edition used throughout this article

56

Really? We need an acrostic to remember those ten punishing plagues visited on the Egyptians?

Ma'aseh Nissim, the 18th-century commentary by Polish scholar Rabbi Yaakov Lorberbaum asks the question, "What purpose is served in grouping the plagues together in this fashion, and abbreviating them?" He explains that each acrostic group is a subset of the ten plagues, "with the final plague [in each group] a climax" to those that preceded them, in theory to teach a particular lesson, working up to the last grouping, Ba'achav - hail, locusts, darkness, the death of the first born - acknowledging that the plagues weren't "...just chance or a product of the astrological signs (Mazel), but the actual hand of God."

Rabbi Yehuda makes it clear: the plagues were both fearsome and personal, a punishment meted out by God on the Egyptian people. The ten plagues are then followed by a famous game of numbers, a sort of Haggadic gematria, where words and phrases are assigned numeric values and special powers. Rabbi Yossi Haglili, Rabbi Eliezer and Rabbi Akiva outdo themselves proving that each of the plagues is really a multiple plague representing God's strength, might, and anger.

Rabbi Yossi speaks of the hand and finger of God, saying:

אֱמוֹר מֵעַתָּה: בְּמִצְרַיִם לָקוּ עֶשֶׂר מַכּוֹת
וְעַל הַיָּם לָקוּ חֲמִשִּׁים מַכּוֹת

"You can say from here that in Egypt, they were struck with ten plagues and at the Sea they were struck with fifty plagues."

Rabbi Eliezer builds on this idea of God's anger, wrath, and fury, saying,

אֱמוֹר מֵעַתָּה: בְּמִצְרַיִם לָקוּ אַרְבָּעִים מַכּוֹת
וְעַל הַיָּם לָקוּ מָאתַיִם מַכּוֹת

"You can say from here that in Egypt, they were struck with forty plagues and at the Sea they were struck with two hundred plagues."

Finally, Rabbi Akiva takes God's anger the furthest, saying that each plague was a multiple of five,

יְשַׁלַּח־בָּם חֲרוֹן אַפּוֹ, עֶבְרָה וָזַעַם וְצָרָה, מִשְׁלַחַת מַלְאֲכֵי רָעִים. חֲרוֹן אַפּוֹ – אַחַת, עֶבְרָה – שְׁתַּיִם, וָזַעַם – שָׁלוֹשׁ, וְצָרָה – אַרְבַּע, מִשְׁלַחַת מַלְאֲכֵי רָעִים – חָמֵשׁ. אֱמוֹר מֵעַתָּה: בְּמִצְרַיִם לָקוּ חֲמִשִּׁים מַכּוֹת וְעַל הַיָּם לָקוּ חֲמִשִּׁים וּמָאתַיִם מַכּוֹת.

"[God] sent upon them the fierceness of [God's] anger, wrath, and fury, and trouble, a sending of messengers of evil. 'The fierceness of His anger' [corresponds to] one; 'wrath' [brings it to] two; 'and fury' [brings it to] three; 'and trouble' [brings it to] four; 'a sending of messengers of evil' [brings it to] five. You can say from here that in Egypt, they were struck with fifty plagues and at the Sea, they were struck with two hundred and fifty plagues."

This year, I read this section with dread, thinking of the murderous rage wrought upon Israel on October 7th. Hamas's messengers of evil unleashed fierce anger, wrath, and fury on innocent Israeli civilians, on soldiers cowering in their beds, on lovers of music taking cover in bomb shelters or hiding in fields, on families in their safe rooms. How many plagues were visited on those caught up in the bloodlust on October 7th?

Hamas's messengers of evil incited their own, Gazan civilians, to join their murderous rampage - a plague for sure. They left those who sheltered at home unprotected - another plague - without the food, water, and physical protection needed to survive the obvious wrath of a country invaded by a neighboring enemy, its citizenry plundered, living people taken as hostage, dead bodies taken as war booty. The plagues of war that followed, along with injury, death and destruction, for Gazans, and for Israeli families who've lost loved ones on October 7th and onward, from rocket fire, or as family members of soldiers defending their homeland, have multiplied the pain felt by so many.

Plagues, plagues, and more plagues. How many plagues really? Who can count them?

The emotional, physical, and existential pain of knowing that peace or something akin to living as neighbors seems more elusive than ever? It's a plague to be sure. Of many multiples.

"A plague o' both your house," says Mercutio, in Romeo and Juliet, right before he dies, struck down in a swordfight that didn't have to happen. He curses both houses, Montague and Capulet, instead of preaching reconciliation. Sadly, in that story, it takes more death and sadness before the families find their way forward.

This Pesach, as we read through the plagues, let's talk through their anger, along with the pain of this year's plagues, pain that for many is still part of their lives and may continue to be so. Can we follow the plague of loss with healing-talk and trusting-talk - between ourselves as a Jewish community divided, and beyond our communal borders, to those enemies of our people. Only then, as a people who pray for peace, can we find the bravery needed to overcome these endless plagues of violence, of wrath, and of hatred. Bravery is the only way towards talking together, crying together, and yes, making peace together.

Beth Steinberg is co-founder and co-director of Shutaf and is the artistic director of Theater in the Rough in Jerusalem.

A Plague Poem
Rabbi Margaret Frisch Klein

"The Egyptians were drowning in the sea. At the
same time, the angels wanted to sing before God,
and the Lord, God, said to them: *'My creations are
drowning, and you are singing before me?'*"
                                        - Talmud, Megillah 10

My creatures are drowning...
Why are you singing?
A drop of wine
A drop of blood
Not just 10 for the plagues
Too many drops to count this year
Maybe every year
A drop of wine
A drop of blood
We rejoice with each hostage freed
Out of the narrow places
A drop of wine
A drop of blood
A tunnel is a narrow place
A very narrow place
We weep for each life lost
Child, woman, man
Every Gazan, Every Israeli
Every soldier
Every "non-combatant"

Every victim from any country
Every person
Each created in the image of the Divine
A drop of wine
A drop of blood
We weep for each victim
Each victim of terror
Each victim of sexual assault
Each victim of displacement
Each victim of brutality
Each victim of promises made
And promises shattered
Each victim searching for water
And searching for food
And searching for safety
Searching for school
And searching for healing
Each victim of fear
We pray that soon
All will be out of the tunnels
Out of the narrow places
God admonished the angels
"My creatures are drowning, and you rejoice?"
A drop of wine
A drop of blood
Too, too many drops this year
We cannot sing this year
Next year may all be free
Out of the narrow places.

Why does Torah give no command to rejoice during Pesach?

Because the Egyptians died during Pesach. And similarly, do you find that although we read the [entire] Hallel on each of the seven days of Sukkot, on Pesach we read the entire Hallel only on the first day and on the night preceding it. Why? Because of this quote: "Do not gloat at the fall of your enemy." (Proverbs 24:17).

Rabbi Margaret Frisch Klein is the Rabbi of Congregation Kneseth Israel in Elgin, IL. She was ordained by the Academy for Jewish Religion.

Hardened Hearts

Rabbi Linda Shriner-Cahn

A field of hearts
Cracked open.
Hardened

Shards covering an open field.
Unrecognizable
Once beating, caring giving
Rage breaking them asunder.

Who did this?
Why?
Who will mend all of the brokenness?
The pain, the anguish

Pharoah heart hardened,
His own will?
Maybe not
Blind to his people,
Wanting glory above all else
Refusing to lose
Winning at all costs

Until the abyss
The death of a child
Love and loss intertwined.

It feels like the abyss.
Is staring at us

In this very moment

Stepping back
Holding one another
Taking one step backward
Inch by painful inch

The hearts begin to soften.
And healing becomes an option.

Rabbi Linda Shriner-Cahn is rabbi at Congregation Tehillah in Riverdale, NY. She is an alumna of the Academy for Jewish Religion.

Lo Rak Zeh:
A Response to Dayenu

Dr. Leah Cassorla

Not Only This	Lo Rak Zeh	לא רק זה
The truth is:	HaEmet Hi:	האמת היא:
We were not satisfied	Lo Dayeinu	לא דיינו
Because we didn't know	Ki Lo Yadanu	כי לא ידענו
All the things we wanted	Kol Mah Sh'Ratzinu	כל מה שרצינו
What we needed	Mah Sh'Hitztarachnu	מה שהצטרכנו
What we would experience	Mah Sh'Na'avor	מה שנעבור
We were not satisfied,	Lo Dayeinu	לא דיינו,
But we gave thanks	Aval Hodanu	אבל הודנו
The Truth is:	HaEmet Hi:	האמת היא:
We were not satisfied	Lo Dayeinu	לא דיינו
Because we didn't see	Ki Lo Ra'inu	כי לא ראינו
How hard it is	Kamah Zeh Kasheh	כמה זה קשה
This ache	Ha'Ke'ev Ha'Zeh	הכאב הזה
All that will be	Kol Mah Sh'Yihyeh	כל מה שיהיה
We were not satisfied,	Lo Dayeinu	לא דיינו,
But we gave thanks	Aval Hodanu	אבל הודנו

Th truth is:	*HaEmet Hi:*	האמת היא:
We are still	*HaYom Od Lo*	היום עוד לא
not satisfied	*Dayeinu*	דיינו
We still ask	*Adayin*	עדיין מבקשים
	M'Vakshim	
Still wait	*Adayin*	עדיין מחכים
	M'Khakim	
Still search	*Adayin*	עדיין מחפשים
	M'Khapsim	
Because until	*Ki Ad Sh'Hem*	כי עד שהם
they return	*Khozrim*	חוזרים
We cannot	*Lo Dayeinu*	לא דיינו
be satisfied		
But we give	*Aval Hodanu*	אבל הודנו
thanks		

Dr. Leah Cassorla is a Kol-Bo student at the Academy for Jewish Religion, and serves as Cantor and Educational Director at the Melville Jewish Center in New York.

One Must See Oneself

Chen Artzi Saror
English Translation: Rabbi Karen Reiss Medwed, PhD
adapted by Rabbi Robert Scheinberg, PhD

One must see
oneself as one who
came out of Be'eri.
Out of K'far Aza.
Out of S'derot.
Out of Ofakim.
Remember and do
not forget
until the final day.
Not to seed more
fear: but to ready
our hope.
Elderly will again
sit on the lawns of
Be'eri,

חייב אדם לראות את עצמו כאילו
הוא יצא מבארי. מכפר עזה.
משדרות. מאופקים. לזכור ולא
לשכוח עד ליום אחרון. לא בדי להזין
את הפחד: להפך, בדי לבונן את
התקווה. עוד יישבו זקנים וזקנות
במדשאות בארי, ורחובות העיר
שדרות ימלאו ילדים וילדות
משחקים. הבתים השרופים ייצבעו
מחדש, הנירים ייחרשו והעגבניות
ייקטפו. האיום הקיומי יוסר. זוהי לא
נבואת נחמה, זוהי תוכנית עבודה.

חן ארצי סרור

The streets of S'derot will fill with children
playing.
Torched houses will be painted over,
Plowed fields will be furrowed
and tomatoes will be picked.
The existential threat will be removed.
This is not a prophecy of consolation
THIS is our next agenda

71

Generation Gaps

Rabbi David Ehrenkranz

My grandfather didn't like my father's music
And my father didn't like my music.
We disagreed about the lyrics.
And the order
And the speed of the notes.

Mixed together at the right tempo
In the right octave
Our ears would allow sound
To touch our hearts, sending us
To places only known to us.

But just as every lock
Has its own
Combination
So too did our
Respective hearts.

Coltrane stirred my father's
But not my grandfather's.
The Beatles stirred mine
But not my father's. And Frank Sinatra
Stirred my grandfather's and no one else's.

There were rarities that moved us all.
Billie Holliday, Peggy Lee and
Nat King Cole. But even then we
Would not admit to each other that our souls

73

Were being plucked by the same hands of these
singing prophets.

But sometimes
The words would bring us together
Like the Seder
When we all sang for the one baby goat
Who we all wished to protect.

Prayer for Guidance and Help
Rabbi Dr. Jo David

What does it mean to feel a personal experience of the exodus from Egypt? Throughout history, all mass migrations have been composed of a "mixed multitude." Who were the people who left their homes? What truly motivated them? What were their hopes and dreams as they traveled toward the Promised Land?

The modern state of Israel is not just a symbol of the biblically promised Jewish homeland. It is the literal home of the world-wide Jewish community created against the backdrop of the Holocaust. The state of Israel is a guarantee that the Jewish people will never be homeless again. The threat that the October 7 War represents is not "merely" that of pain and suffering, but of a return to homelessness for the Jewish people. It is a terrifying thought — that Jews living today might have to undergo an exodus from our homeland in our lifetime.

How can we respond to this threat? Few of us are able to pick up a weapon and fight on the front lines. The scope of suffering goes beyond nationalistic ideologies and challenges our compassion and our resources. Feelings of fear, helplessness and hopelessness are overwhelming and disabling. What are we to do?

In times of trouble, Psalm 121 urges us to turn for strength and guidance to the One who is the maker of heaven and earth. A famous teaching of the great spiritual master, Rebbe Nachman of Bratslav, is that one should make time each day to commune with

75

nature and speak out loud, from the heart to God. What connects both these ideas is the concept of creating a focus for prayer. When we feel helpless and hopeless, we ask, "What can I do?" It is with this question in mind that I offer the following prayer.

Prayer for Guidance and Help

Please note: It is traditional to direct a prayer to the Divine in one of God's many aspects, as in one of the most common introductions, "Baruch ata ...." In order to make this prayer meaningful to as many people as possible, a *specific* introduction has not been written for this prayer. It has been left for each individual to supply the direction if such direction is desired.

עֲשֵׂה אֶת חֲזוֹנְךָ לַחֲזוֹנִי
עֲשֵׂה אֶת בִּנָתְךָ לַבִּנָתִי
עֲשֵׂה אֶת כֹּחֲךָ לְכֹחִי
כְּדֵי שֶׁאוּכַל לַעֲשׂוֹת אֶת עֲבוֹדָתְךָ בָּעוֹלָם.

Ah-seh et cha-zon-n'cha la-cha-zo-ni
Ah-seh et bi-na-t'cha la bi-na-ti
Ah-seh et koh-cha-cha la-choh-hee
K'day sheh-oh-chal la-ah-soat et ah-voh-dah-t'cha
bah-oh-lahm.

Make Your sight my sight,
Make Your wisdom my wisdom,
Make your strength my strength
So that I may do your work in the world.
Amen.

Rabbi Dr. Jo David is a writer, teacher, interfaith counselor, and life-cycle officiant. She was ordained as a rabbi under the auspices of the Academy for Jewish Religion in New York.

מצה
Matzah

Angry Chametz
A Meditation Before
We Talk About Matzah
Rabbi Dan Ornstein

Rabbi Avraham Yehoshua Heschel (1748-1825) was known
by his nom de plume, the Oheiv Yisrael, "The Lover of the
people of Israel." (He was also the great, great grandfather
of Rabbi Abraham Heschel.) Stories abound of his
gentleness, deep love and compassion for all his fellow Jews.
Here is one story, as retold by Rabbi Moshe Shlomo
Friedman, the Rebbe (grand rabbi) of the Boyaner Hasidic
dynasty in New York:

Rabbi Pinchas of Koretz was extremely strict
about the laws concerning the removal of
chametz, leavened food, on Pesach. The Oheiv
Yisrael was less strict. One Pesach, one of
Pinchas's grandsons came to visit the Oheiv
Yisrael's family. Because he observed his
grandfather's stringencies so scrupulously and
zealously, he got into a great deal of angry
conflict with his host's family during the holiday.
The Oheiv Yisrael finally took the young man
aside and said to him, "You should know that
anger is a form of chametz which is forbidden all
year round."

The Oheiv Yisrael playfully but roundly
criticized the young man by alluding to a
halachic (legal) rule that he would have known:
chametz which remains in a Jew's possession
during Pesach is forbidden during the rest of the

year. The biblical prohibition against even owning (let alone eating) chametz on Pesach is so strict that the Talmudic sages forbade the use of this kind of chametz for all time. The rabbi was also hinting at a common trope in Rabbinic and later Hasidic literature. It compares the overly fastidious, arrogant, and angry sides of our personalities – the parts of us that are "puffed up with pride" - to leavened, risen bread. On Pesach, we try to free ourselves from the "spiritual Egypt" of our anger and arrogance, to achieve the humility-that-shuns-harshness symbolized by the lowly, unleavened matzah. Some Talmudic and Hasidic teachings often go even further, shunning *all* anger at all times of the year.

Our teacher was telling his young guest: "Your fastidious religious piety isn't pious; it isn't even religious. You're busy being so holy and angrily judging everyone in my family about chametz. Can't you see what the chametz of your anger is doing to you and to the rest of us? You think you're celebrating Pesach? Nonsense! You're stuck in Egypt, now *and* year-round."

Angry quibbling over rituals is incomparable with life-and-death conflict. Still, this story speaks to us as we celebrate our first Pesach after October 7. Israel was severely traumatized by the toxic, religiously fueled hatred, and rage of Hamas. Our people rightly responded with a rage born of deep vulnerability and a steadfast refusal to let such barbarity go unpunished. Yet, to paraphrase Robert Frost, "rage leads onto rage." So much suffering and destruction fueled by hate and deep mistrust are bleeding Jews and Palestinians to death, in different yet equally poisonous ways. The chametz of anger and hopelessness is bloating our two peoples to the point where we risk exploding.

How can we cool this rage and bring peace – the ultimate exodus from Egypt – to our peoples and even to our angry planet? We lack the power of international leaders to change things globally. Yet taking our cue from the Oheiv Yisrael, we recognize that the personal is global. Deflating destructive anger on a world scale begins with each of us, who are microcosms of humanity. For examples, we have control over how we speak to each other, especially when talking about polarizing topics such as Israel and Palestine. We have control over how we treat each other, as enemies whose opinions are seen as weapons, or as friends who love each other while agreeing to disagree. We have control over whether we approach others in the community with courtesy and curiosity or with our fingers on the proverbial trigger. We decide what to put into the world.

At this point in the seder we lift the matzah and ask: "What is the reason that our ancestors ate this matzah?" We might also ask: "*How can we replace our angry chametz with the matzah of our humility?*"

Rabbi Dan Ornstein is the rabbi at Congregation Ohav Shalom in Albany, NY.

Matzah of Healing
(*Refuah*)

The first and second nights of Passover fall on April 22 and April 23, 2024. At a traditional seder, three pieces of matzah are used to represent the three groups of Jews: Kohanim (high priests), Levi'im (those who assist the Kohanim) and Yisraelim (all others). This year, we ask that you add a fourth matzah to represent a "matzah of healing" and read the paragraphs included below. Hold up the fourth matzah as you read:

This is the matzah of healing.

As we begin our seder, we take pride in the growing *achdut* (unity) about the importance of Israel today. The expression "all of Israel is responsible for one another" is truer today than ever before. The war has brought Jews from around the world together in their support and love of Israel.

Tonight we add this fourth matzah to our table to represent the matzah of healing (*refuah*). This is the matzah that exemplifies our hopes for a healthy future for the Jewish nation. We recognize the need for all of us to *end the silence* too often felt in trying times such as these. We hope that with support from others, those that need it will have the opportunity and time to heal. Just as we have shared in the sadness and trauma of October 7, we look forward to a better future. We hope this matzah will bring us healing, strength, comfort, and renewal.

May the seder tables of our people be filled with reunited families and may those who are not with us be remembered with love. We pray that all those wounded by the war will achieve a *Refuah shleimah* (a complete recovery) through treatment, time, love, and the observance of our ancient traditions.

Let our *matzah* of *refuah* bring healing, joy, hope, comfort, and renewal to all those celebrating Pesach around the world. And may we continue to go from strength to strength.

Am Yisrael Chai!

Upon completion of the reading, add the matzah to the other three that you've set aside.

Produced by the Jewish Education Department of HADASSAH, THE WOMEN'S ZIONIST ORGANIZATION OF AMERICA, INC. ©2024 Hadassah, The Women's Zionist Organization of America, Inc. Hadassah and the H logo are registered trademarks of Hadassah, The Women's Zionist Organization of America, Inc.

מרור
Maror

Lisa Link, "Maror"

Being an Egyptian
Rabbi Anat Katzir

Almost every year, at some point when we read the plagues, after remembering how bad it was to be an Israelite slave and finding hope in the faith and endurance of my people, I think to myself. Yeah, being a slave in Egypt must have been awful, and we had Moses, and Aaron, and Miriam, and maybe God.

But what was is like to be an Egyptian?

I'm not thinking about the hard- hearted Pharaoh or one of the fancy Egyptians, with headdresses and makeup, who lived in the palace and had bowls of jewelry they could taunt Israelite captured babies with.

I mean the simple Egyptians, that worked in the field. Whose crops were eaten by locusts, whose livestock died from disease. They sat there scratching their heads, perhaps from lice, perhaps because they couldn't understand why all these horrible things were happening to them. What must have been their pain as they held their eldest children in their arms in that final plague… Were there no uninvolved Egyptians?

As I sit and eat the bitter herb and charoset, and pray for freedom for children of Israel, I also wonder what food symbolizes the pain of those who have no choice? What is the food of the voiceless, caught up in someone else's war?

Maybe brussels sprouts. Bitter, but if given time, and cared for properly, can become something good. Or maybe because sprouts have hope.

מקור החיים, מקור הרחמים, מי ייתן ונבורך בחמלה ובתקווה.

Source of Life, Source of Mercy, may we be blessed with compassion and with hope.

Rabbi Anat Levin-Katzir is the Director of Education at Kol Dorot, a Reform Jewish Community in Oradell, NJ. She is an alumna of the Academy for Jewish Religion.

Unable To Remember Which Terrorist Attack, The Poet Still Recalls

Danny Siegel

We are gunned down again.
(How they say we love wallowing pig-like
in the swill of self-pitied victimhood.)
A 6-year-old. A 3-year-old.
Too dead too soon
to die with dignity.

It feels like, today,
The Grand Old Pioneers will never die in peace,
surrounded by their Sabras

          Motti (dead, age 4)
     and Rachel (8)
   and Avi (5)

                     also dead.
                     all so dead.

This previously published poem appears with the author's permission.

Shared Sorrow

Alex Lazarus-Klein

The wounds I carry are mine
but they are yours as well

The knife that entered twists
through us both simultaneously

I watched your smile turn
my color pale in shadowed silence

My breath broken pain freed
alive in my body as well as yours

How do we heal anger held
like unpunctured blisters raw

No the wounds that I carry
are also yours

Even if you had nothing to do
with them sit with me

Unsheath the harm and let flow
all that needs to pour out

In anguish may we bind our lives
smeared with love

In time I will explain but you still
may never understand

Nod nonetheless acknowledge
our pain is intertwined

In that silence
spit out your tears

Rabbi Alex Lazarus-Klein is rabbi at Congregation Shir
Shalom in Williamsville, NY.

Where? How?

Chana Stein

איכה

Where are you?

Who are you?

How can you?

When you were born, they said " מברוך"", called you "Blessing",

Your father whispered tender prayers into your newborn ear

Your mother dripped honeyed water so that you would begin your life with sweetness

Your family gathered together in celebration only for you, a miracle, a new joy,

איכה

Where is he?

Where are you?

 How can you?

When you were five, your smile shone as you kicked your ball to the boy you played with- who he is does not matter.

Was this you? Or were you taught that hate is more powerful than love?

Who are you, then? Who are you now?

Your grin lit the room and laughter filled the space when, at nine, his joke tickled your mood.

Where has he gone, this boy, this child of love?

Was that you? Or did you learn to hold the weapon?

Who are you, then? Who are you now?

How did this man of anger enter, and destroy?

How did this hate consume you,my child, my friend, my brother?

איכה
Where have you gone?
You, Youth, with your pockets filled for the first time,
your eyes viewing a future alight with possibilities,
love, life, beauty
You, Man, with your arms embracing your bride, the
entire village carried into your welcoming home.
You, Father, gently cupping her growing belly
Where did you find this madness?
You, Anger, with fire in your heart
You, Hate, with destruction in your eyes
You, Brother, where are you?
You, Brother, how could you?

איכה
I have been taught what you have been taught- That
my enemy is Wrong
I have learned what you have learned - That my enemy
is Evil
I have seen what you have seen- That my enemy is
Other
And that You are my enemy
Are you Other, friend?
Are you Evil?
Are you wrong, brother?
I did not see you this way until you came into my home
and did what is other, wrong and Evil-
Where is my brother?

איכה
Who will you become?
How will you be the person you were?
After you have cut this baby's head from his body, how
will you look into your daughter's eyes?
After you have burned this family until their screams
stopped , how will you hear your brother's pain?
After you have stolen this grandmother-her papery
skin shrinking away from your rough hands, how will
you hold your mother without feeling them both?

95

After this madness, this hate, this destruction,
After you have become death, how, my brother, How
will you return?

איכה

Where are You?
I reach out to you: where are you?
Will we meet, talk, touch?
Can we be? Brother? Friend? דוד?
I fear you- I fear for you.
Where is your heart?
Where is your soul?

איכה
Where are we?

I reach out to you and cannot touch your hand as the
bloods of my beloveds drip down and my tears pour
down my face.
My friend, my brother
Return to life
so that we can continue together.
Return to yourself

איכה
הנני
I am here

Chana Stein is a rabbinical student at the Academy for
Jewish Religion. She is an education professional and a
storyteller.

שְׁפֹךְ חֲמָתְךָ

Pour Out Your Wrath

Deborah Ugoretz, "Pour Out Thy Wrath"

Opening the Door
in Dark Times

Rabbi Gordon Tucker, PhD

There is a moment in the Passover Seder that I always find very poignant, though I suspect it is not for the same reason that it moves so many others. It is the opening of the door for Elijah, just after we've given thanks for the festival meal, and before completing the uplifting songs of Hallel. Elijah is anticipated as the herald of the Messiah, and so opening the door, especially at the Feast of Redemption, is to welcome the long-awaited Redemption.[14]

The poignancy of that ritual moment for me is, alas, downbeat in nature. For we know, by induction from centuries of experience, including the worst of times, that it is nearly certain that there will be no one at the door. We may indulge a fantasy, imagining an invisible visitor somehow sipping wine.

But invisible redeemers, though they may fascinate and delight our children, are no substitute for the real thing that the world so desperately needs. And so, I sadly see the

---

[14] Such is the understanding of the practice by the Maharil in the 14th-15th centuries.

opening of the door as an inevitable dashing of hope.

What can the mood be this year when we open our doors? Can we, the unfortunate witnesses to the face of evil that *"devoured Jacob and desolated his home"* sing words of welcome to the invisible Elijah without those words turning to ash in our mouths?

The German scholar Daniel Goldschmidt, in his commentary on the Haggadah, took note of a paradox inherent in the Passover eve liturgy from the start. For the Seder came into existence after the destruction of the Second Temple. And yet, as the Mishnah tells us, the liturgy included Hallel and a "Blessing of Song". Goldschmidt commented as follows:

> "The praises of God contained in the Hallel, gratitude for all the kindnesses shown to God's people, rescuing and protecting them from danger, must have spoken to the post-destruction generations as sardonic humor (literally: *mocking the unfortunate*)."

It surely was that for so many generations of Jews who had experienced poverty, persecutions, and pogroms. And just as surely for us, in the wake of October 7, the dissonance between our fear and despair on the one hand, and the triumphalism in the words of the Haggadah on the other, may be difficult to bear.

What, then, can we do? It is perhaps instructive that the opening of the door is followed by a recitation of verses beginning with lines from Psalm 79:

שְׁפֹךְ חֲמָתְךָ אֶל־הַגּוֹיִם אֲשֶׁר לֹא יְדָעוּךָ וְעַל־מַמְלָכוֹת אֲשֶׁר בְּשִׁמְךָ לֹא קָרָאוּ... כִּי אָכַל אֶת־יַעֲקֹב וְאֶת־נָוֵהוּ הֵשַׁמּוּ.

"Pour out your fury on the nations that do not know you.....for they have devoured Jacob and desolated his home."

To whom are these words addressed?

The conventional answer is that they are addressed to God, who is asked to inflict retribution on those who have harmed God's people. But perhaps we can imagine the "you" here to be each celebrant at the Seder reading the Haggadah.

That is, after we see the emptiness at the hoped-for door of redemption, we are prompted to pour out *our own* fury at what the world can inflict. We need the catharsis of expressing rage at the violation and destruction of human bodies, the cruel holding of hostages who have yet to be brought out from darkness to light, and the crushing of the dream that in a sovereign and armed Jewish state such things were safely in the past.

So yes, the expression of rage at brutality suffered by our people is not out of place. It is natural, and does no good when it is kept in. But there is one more crucial element in this cathartic moment that must not be missed. For the anger to which we give expression is placed just before the third

103

psalm of the Hallel, Psalm 115. The opening words are:

לֹא לָנוּ, ה', לֹא לָנוּ,
כִּי לְשִׁמְךָ תֵּן כָּבוֹד

"Not for us, Lord, not for us,
but rather for the glory of Your name."

Goldschmidt believed that the cathartic verses of anger were intentionally placed here as a preamble to Psalm 115. And that juxtaposition, as we absorb not only October 7 but also the war in the ensuing months, conveys a very weighty and timely message: We are given leave to express our wrath at what the pre-messianic world can mete out, but then we are immediately reminded that the anger must translate itself into acts that are not about our aggrandizement or felt need for revenge, but solely to further the kind of world that gives testimony to God's presence and purposes.

As the door opens this year, let us both testify to the truth of our shredded emotions, and yet work for the truth of God's purposes for the world and its inhabitants.

Rabbi Gordon Tucker, PhD is the Vice Chancellor for Religious Life and Engagement at the Jewish Theological Seminary.

The Fifth Pour

Pam Ehrenkranz

There's a lot of pouring at a seder, most notably, four cups of wine. Yet there is one more pouring: *Shfoch chamat'cha* - A request for God to pour out the Divine anger against the nations that have "consumed Jacob and laid waste his home,"[15] and to destroy them.

An out and out call for God to destroy our enemies. Feeling relatively safe and secure, many of us have tried to soften this seemingly gratuitous call for anger by adding a prayer for the righteous gentiles (one written 400 years before the Holocaust), or to use this moment to remember the victims of the Shoah. We have, over the years, tried to find ways to explain this ancient text as a lens into the period of time in which it was written and to distance ourselves from it because it makes us uncomfortable. I have, for years, always looked for a poem or prayer to offset this passage at our seder.

But this year's seder will be different from all my other seders: I will say *shfoch chamat'cha* with no additions, no qualifications. Avoiding saying this paragraph is a failure of imagination, and most certainly, a failure of empathy. The rabbis composed this paragraph in response to the crushing destruction of the Crusades. The reference to nations who "know not" God is a direct inference to Pharoah and vicious leaders like him. Softening the Haggadic text means that we have missed the

15 Ps. 79:6-7

entire point of the seder, which is to empathize — to empathize with those who endured slavery and those who experienced the redemption from Egypt. Why then, shouldn't we empathize with the Jews who suffered devastating loss throughout the generations? This is the year to own this painful prayer, the year to ask God to mete out justice and carefully pour His wrath on those who have been barbaric and murderous to the Jewish people. To those who have laid waste to their homes, to their kibbutzim, and who consumed the lives of the innocent. To pour his wrath out on those who have held our people hostage and committed heinous acts of sexual violence against women.

And while we ask God for this, we open the door: For Elijah, for redemption, for hope for a better future. This year, we must emulate the God to whom we pray. We have to emerge from the seder ready to channel our anger, to speak out and stand up against rampant antisemitism. We need to publicly pour out our anger carefully against those who earned it, not shy away from seeking their destruction and our continued existence — while keeping the door open, all the while, negotiating for peace. Elijah's cup sits poured, ready and waiting, to welcome an era when it will indeed be impossible, much less a failure, to imagine *shfoch chamat'cha*'s necessity.

Pam Ehrenkranz is a rabbinical student at the Academy for Jewish Religion. She is the CEO of UJA-JCC Greenwich.

106

Speak Out

Rabbi Avi Orlow
adapted from Martin Niemöller

First they came for the Zionists, and I did not
speak out—because being anti-Zionist is not
Antisemitic.

Then they killed civilians and took hostages, and
I did not speak out- because Israelis are
colonialists.

Then they raped Jewish women, and I did not
speak out- because I did not believe the victims
or the bodycams.

Then they came for the Jews in traditional attire,
and I did not speak out—because they chose to
set themselves apart.

Then they came for the Jews who dress like me,
and I did not speak out—because they are white
and are excluded from our DEI policy.

Then they came for me—and there was no one
left to speak for me.

The west is next.

Rabbi Avi Orlow is Vice President of Program and
Innovation at Foundation for Jewish Camp.

Shfoch Chamat'cha

Rabbi Beth Naditch

Throughout our liturgy, we hopefully include "*Erech apayim*," the quality of being slow to anger, in the Thirteen Attributes of God.[16] Most humans, as individuals and collectively, viscerally know the experience of being the target of another's anger, an experience which can range from uncomfortable to frightening. Fraught with vulnerability, unpredictability, and potential lack of safety, many people strive to avoid being either the aggressor or the recipient of anger. The ideal of slowness to anger both for God and for we human beings who strive to live in the image of God is one to which we hold fast in more peaceful times.

It is alarmingly easy, however, to carry the messaging of *erech apayim* a step forward and slip into the mindset that anger should *always* be subdued or suppressed. In most years, this passage in our Haggadah, with its unabashed embrace of anger towards our enemies, can be a challenging one. In times such as these, however, when the full spectrum of human emotions flow turbulently through our souls in response to horrifying events, suppressing anger would deprive us of critical outlets to process grief, loss, and trauma. Anger, when appropriately directed, is a life-giving force.

---

[16] Ex. 34:6

As Abraham Joshua Heschel taught,

> "Like fire, (anger) may be a blessing as well as a fatal thing - reprehensible when associated with malice, morally necessary as resistance to malice. Both alternatives are fraught with danger. (Anger's) complete suppression even the face of outbursts of evil may amount to surrender and capitulation, while its unrestrained drive may end in disaster. Anger may touch off deadly explosives, while the complete absence of anger stultifies moral sensibility."

When *Shfoch Chamat'cha* was added to the Haggadah is not certain, but it is thought to have appeared in the Middle Ages during other times of persecution. What a gift that our ancestors have left us with language, borrowed from Psalms, compelling to them as they grappled with their own experiences of persecution. Their words offer us a map of how to navigate the experiences of our times that demand response.

We do not have to wrestle with new words to hold our own anger, distress, and fear, as they have blessed us with theirs. In articulating their experiences, our ancestors have accompanied us into ours, leaving us resourced, and most important, not alone. We are provoked to cry out for God's protection, as our ancestors did in Egypt. We are asked to take on the challenge of beseeching a God who poured out wrath in Egypt on those who mistreated us, a God we call on to have our backs when we are grieving and furious and at the limits of what we as human can do to fight evil. We are invited to explore what God's protection looks like in our time, when it does not come in the form of plagues or large-scale miracles like the closing of the sea over those who pursued us.

This year, I am struck by the pageantry of this passage, in which we are instructed to open our doors and intone these words, publicly, into the street. What a privilege it is for those who have the freedom to open our doors in safety without fearing harm from outside, and how suddenly fragile that freedom feels. How dramatically different this seemingly normal experience - opening our doors - is from the hours and hours our people hid in safe rooms in the South of Israel, gripping the door handles and barring them shut with their bodies while Hamas rampaged inside their homes. How wildly distinct from the experience of our college students on many campuses at this moment. This year, the Jewish people has not needed to wait for the Passover seder to imagine our lives as slaves - we know that it could be any one of us captive in Gaza, and we weep for our brothers and sisters stolen away and suffering.

This year, I move past slowness to anger with every news report, and hope that intoning these words might help to purge the fury and fear from my own body, even temporarily. Next year, may we all be free from captivity, from fear, from fury. Next year, may we all know safety and security and have no more need for these words.

Shfoch

Rabbi David Seidenberg, PhD

> Pour Your fierce anger onto the nations that did not know You and on the governments that did not call in Your name. For it has eaten Jacob and made his habitat desolate. (Psalms 79:6-7)
>
> Pour on them Your fury and make You burning anger grip them. (Psalms 69:25)
>
> Pursue in anger and destroy them from under YHVH's heavens. (Lament. 3:66)

It is right to feel anger when we think about the trauma of Jewish history and the recent traumas of October 7and its aftermath. Repressing or denying our fierce anger is unhealthy. That fire held tightly inside can consume us, as it says, "it has eaten Jacob." But feeling it as a desire for vengeance, and acting that out, is unholy. Anger, when hardened into a desire for vengeance, can become vicious, can re-traumatize us again and again, can turn victim into victimizer. Instead, the Haggadah invites us to entrust God with our anger, and to ask Hashem to take over our anger and find its right use in the world.

This can only happen after we are willing to let go, to release even the most justified, firmly rooted anger, anger that is born out of grief and loss. A way to do this: open the door, step outside, recite *Sh'foch Chamat'cha* aloud, declaiming it to the world. If you've collected the wine or grape juice that was poured out during the ten plagues, upturn the bowl and pour it out onto the ground. We can let God take our anger and pour it out onto the ground, to be soaked up by the earth. For the earth has power to heal plagues and transmute anger. Even our very worst feelings can be turned into something fertile and life-giving, if we can call on the essential goodness of this Creation and its Creator, the "tov m'od", the very goodness, that is the mark of Creation itself.

Rabbi David Seidenberg, PhD is the Creator/Director at neohasid.org.

Pour out your wrath on the Others (who are your enemy)

Rabbi Sid Schwarz

This year, we need to set a higher bar for the wise child. It is not enough to celebrate this child because s/he dutifully participates in the Seder ritual, unlike her siblings.

I am thinking of the line in the Haggadah that instructs us to pour out our wrath on the "others", who are our enemy. True, many of our festivals tell tales of how Jews overcame an evil ruler. The fact that Jews prevailed becomes evidence of God's love for his chosen people, Israel. It is an effective narrative device: good guys overcome bad guys. Sometimes, it even comes close to being historically accurate. But this year, in the face of the atrocities and slaughter that Hamas perpetrated upon Israelis on October 7th, and then the Israeli assault on Gaza, which has cost the lives of over 30,000 Palestinians, more than half of whom, are women and children, I am hoping that the wise children (and adults) at the Seder table might make a courageous break with the Exodus narrative to reject the demonization of the "other". That narrative becomes a justification to dehumanize that "other" and, once dehumanization happens, innocent people are killed.

As part of our congregation's attempt to explore all sides of the tragic conflict in Israel/Palestine since October 7th, we hosted a visit from an Israeli NGO called Combatants for Peace. The panel included two Israeli Jews and two Palestinians. Each told their story. One of the Palestinians, Sulaiman Khatib, was arrested at age 14 for stabbing two IDF soldiers and trying to steal their weapons. During his 10 years in an Israeli prison, Sulaiman studied the writings of Gandi, Nelson Mandela and Martin Luther King, Jr. and learned that revolutionary change can happen through non-violence. He also learned enough about Jewish history and the tragedy of the Shoah that he realized that the Jews, who, he was taught, were his enemies, had also suffered greatly and that Israel was the Jewish people's refuge.

Chen Alon's grandfather escaped the death camps of Poland during the Shoah and made his way to Israel. Chen was proud to put on an IDF uniform and protect the State of Israel from her enemies, as did his father during the 1967 Six-Day War. And yet, Chen started to see things as a reservist during the First Intifada that troubled his conscience—arresting a 10-year old Palestinian boy for being a "suspected terrorist"; destroying the home of a Palestinian family because they did not have the right permit to add a balcony to their second floor living area; preventing a car driven by a Palestinian from bringing sick children to the hospital in Bethlehem because they did not have proper papers. Chen came to believe that Israel's occupation of over 3 million Palestinians in the West Bank was ethically indefensible. He joined a small group of Israelis who refused to serve in the IDF as a matter of conscience.

Both Sulaiman and Chen manifested a form of courage that is suggested by the Mishnah:

אֵיזֶהוּ גִבּוֹר? הַכּוֹבֵשׁ אֶת יִצְרוֹ.

Who is a hero? The one who can
subdue his/her evil instincts.

(Pirke Avot 4:1)

Chen and Sulaiman rejected the narratives of their respective people which portrayed the other side as "the enemy". They are now part of a small but important constituency of Palestinians and Jews who are committed to the path of mutual respect and a shared society.

May this Pesach inspire many others to become "wise children", who can see beyond the narratives that condemn us to perpetual conflict and violence. Only that way, can we all both envision and then, bring to fruition, the redemption and liberty for all peoples, which is the intent of this festival.

Rabbi Sid Schwarz is the Founding Rabbi of Adat Shalom Reconstructionist Cong., (Bethesda, MD), Director of The Clergy Leadership Incubator (CLI), and author of *Judaism and Justice: The Jewish Passion to Repair the World.*

הלל
Hallel

Hallel Divided Across History

Rabbi Jonah Rank

Tonight, we sing *Hallel*'s six Psalms (113–118), but we split them up. For centuries, the Jewish people have sung Psalms 113 and 114 immediately before reciting a blessing over the night's second cup of wine. By the time we turn to Psalms 115–118, we will have already eaten the festive meal, blessed it, and drunk from our third cup of wine.

On this night, why is *Hallel* broken?

The Portuguese Jewish philosopher Don Isaac Abarbanel (1437–1508) asked the same question in his *Zevach Pesach*.[17] In this essay, Abarbanel built 100 'gates' (שערים, *she'arim*) of queries that sought to deconstruct the oddities of the Passover Seder. Near the end of the work, as he faced his 99th gate—questioning the unusual structure of tonight's Hallel—Abarbanel turned to the Jewish sages who preceded him. His predecessors understood formerly enslaved Israelites as the audience to Psalm 113's opening words:

הַלְלוּ־יָהּ ׀ הַלְלוּ עַבְדֵי יְהֹוָה

Hallelujah! Praise, servants of Adonai!.

---

[17] Abarbanel's זבח פסח, "*The Paschal Sacrifice*," is an extended commentary on the *Maggid* section of the Passover Seder.

This was their song on the night of their liberation. In Abarbanel's words:

באותו לילה לא היינו עבדים לפרעה
ונעשינו עבדים להקדוש ברוך הוא

> "On that night, we were not servants to Pharaoh, but we became servants to the Holy Blessed One."

Our newly freed ancestors of course lived Psalm 114, which opens "בְּצֵאת יִשְׂרָאֵל מִמִּצְרָיִם - *amidst Israel's escaping from Egypt*" and prominently features water caught up in awe and supernatural occurrences. Psalms 113 and 114 therefore constitute what the sages of old called "הלל המצרי - *Hallel HaMitzri* - the Egyptian Hallel."

For our spiritual forebears, Psalms 113–114 were grounded in a foundational mythical time and place: Egypt, on the eve of our freedom. Psalms 115–118, on the other hand, exist outside the realm of the Exodus alone. Though some of these verses express their intimate familiarity with Jerusalem and the Temple within it, Abarbanel marked these four Psalms as "לעתיד לבוא לזמן גליות," "for a future [moment] to come, in a time of exile."

Tonight, Psalms 113–114 bring us back to the Sea of Reeds, tasting for the first time our own flavor of independence as a people. We had not yet eaten the food of free people.

Freedom is a dish served with sides of responsibilities, obligations, opportunities, misfortunes, and all the developments that shape a nation. Once we have fully digested liberty, there follow the aftertastes, some pleasurable and some uncomfortable. We change our tune at Psalm 115. Time has passed since we were freed, and now new songs fill our hearts.

There, the Promised Land, is the land we love. Even when we cannot be in Israel physically, our souls long to return. In days of war, when the Land of Israel cannot be traversed without risk, our bodies seek to reunite with the land where our people grew up—and so much of the Jewish family still lives there. In an age with a Jewish State, we inhabit not a time of literal exile; however, in moments of fear and violence, the land and its inhabitants barely know one another. War stands in the way, redirecting us all to exile.

Tonight is the breaking point; we have become free again, and that can hurt. *Hallel* must fall apart. Let Psalms 113–114 bring us back to the euphoria of leaving Egypt. Let us sit with freedom and let us swallow. We may cry before we can move forward with Psalms 115–118 but let us not drown in a sea of tears. *Hallel* beckons us to muster our greatest memories of the past and to muster bold hope for the future. Then we can sing a truly united *Hallel*.

L'shanah Haba'ah B'yerushalayim

Rabbi Jonah Rank is President and Rosh Yeshivah at the Hebrew Seminary.

Redemption Song

Rabbi-Cantor Michael McCloskey

When I took that piece of paper,
drenched shirt spilling sweat upon it,
crusty with many washes in the hostel sink
to the sounds of my soul's language spoken by
the religious, the secular, and cats

When I placed it into the wall,
With all the hope and love
Of a people whose heart has always moved
multi-directionally.[18]

In Her[19] apricot hookah smoke,
In the mysterious heaviness of
That prophetic syndrome
She spoke to me.

In the arms of mystic-dreamers, and artists,
In her niggunim,
She beckoned me from my exile,
Toward the land of promise,
And sovereignty
And Jewish pride
And guns.

But the Shulamite[20] maiden is taken up with jackals[21]

---

[18] See HaLevi's poem "לבי במזרח/My Heart is in the East"
[19] Jerusalem and the Shulamite maiden of Song of Songs, coming
from the same verbal root, She's described like "Pillars of smoke
coming out of the wilderness" [Song of Songs 3:6] and is also
compared to a "*tapuach*" which is really an apricot, not an apple,
as they hadn't yet been cultivated in the Ancient Near East.
[20] See Song of Songs
[21] See for example, Lamentations 5:18

from without and within,
Bound by watchmen[22]
Who would trade her and put her in a box
Imprisoned by child-warriors of Solomon's palanquin[23],
David's children with the weapons of Goliath.

She, given as concubine to Pharaoh[24], moans and rages at the fate of her daughters, who wandered her ramparts and citadels[25],
Dreaming of their lover's hand upon the latch[26].

The spring has come and the buds have been pruned[27],
But ungently, with swords[28], pride, and zealotry.
Her children, scattered by the scythe
of violence begetting violence
Left behind and cut off at the rear[29]
Pining in the halls of the wisest lands
Pillaged by the pundits,
Gouged by their gambits

And yet,
I hope…
In the polyphonic sparring
Of pashtanim[30],

---

[22] Song of Songs 5:7
[23] Song of Songs 3:9
[24] See Genesis 12:15
[25] Psalms 122:7
[26] Song of Songs 5:4
[27] Song of Songs 2:12
[28] Isaiah 2:4
[29] Deuteronomy 25:17
[30] The string quartet of plain-contextual commentators featured prominently in our classical commentaries on the weekly Torah portion. They disagreed with one another, often and passionately, yet the contrapuntal opinions of each are preserved on each page of these parashah anthologies called Mikraot Gedolot.

In the wedding hymns of students of Hillel and
Shammai[31]
In reconciliation of brothers and family
Like Isaac and Ishmael
Esau and Jacob
Who mourned their loss,
Crying upon each other's shoulder,
When they could have been biting.
Laughter unbound seeking The Refugee at Be'er
Lahai Roi[32]
Of therapeutic Jerusalem youth-songs[33]
Of a people ready to listen and
Return to shepherding
Stepping aside to see that we're all bushes burning
And reaching out our hands
Like a prince or a princess wading in the bulrushes
Of mothers and fathers who build arks
And mothers and fathers who bring them to shore
Of old-women songsmiths who shake their booty for
liberation[34]
Of sisters who challenge their brothers when they are
wrong[35],
When they build walls,
Of songs and verse and story that inhabit questions
Of we descendants of songwriter-prophets and kings
Who sing, play, and write, and teach them.

Rav Chazzan Michael McCloskey serves at Temple
Emeth in Chestnut Hill, MA.

---

[31] Babylonian Talmud: Yevamot 14b
[32] See Genesis 24:62 and Midrash HaGadol on Parashat Chayyei
Sarah, 62
[33] https://jerusalemyouthchorus.org/
[34] Exodus 15:21
[35] See Miriam's and Aaron's challenge of Moses in Numbers 12.
Some theorize that he had divorced his wife Tzipporah and sent
her away and that the siblings were holding him accountable.

And...

A Prayer for Pesach
Rabbi Lynnda Targan

Presider Over the Universe:

We prayed for peace and the fulfillment of dreams.
And we woke to a nightmare. A nightmare so unreal that we didn't believe it and still can't comprehend the truth.
It happened!
The unimaginable...

Now we are left with the aftermath...
And shock
And questions
And responsibilities
And burdens
And fears
And disbelief
And, And, And...

Please God, as we enter this season of liberation and renewal, we ask that you watch over us and our Israeli brothers and sisters...
That you bring the hostages safely home from the narrow spaces
That you help heal the wounded.
That you offer comfort to the bereaved.
That you offer healing to shattered souls.
That all innocents be protected.
That there are changes in hearts and minds.

That there be love…
That there be peace…
That there be goodness in all of its iterations…
And, And, And…
Amen.

Rabbi Lynnda Targan is an author, teacher, Mussar facilitator, and life cycle officiant. She is an alumna of the Academy for Jewish Religion.

עוד קְצָת A little more

Dana Greitzer-Gotlieb

Translated by Eyal Akiva and Udi Gotlieb

תְּנוּ לִי	Let me
לְהַחֲזִיק	Latch onto
עוֹד קְצָת	A little more of
עוֹלָם	The world
תְּנוּ לִי	Let me be
בַּקֶּצֶב שֶׁלִּי	In my rhythm
בִּתְנוּעָה שֶׁיּוֹדַעַת נַפְשִׁי	In my soul's movement
בְּחָכְמַת כֶּתֶם שֶׁמֶשׁ	In the wisdom of a sunspot
וְגַרְגֵּר חוֹל רָזֶה	And the secret of a grain of sand
תְּנוּ	Let me
שְׁאָרִים מַלְבּוּשִׁי	Thrust my tangled garments
הַפְּרוּם מֵעָפָר וְאָשׁוּב	So dust to ash will soar
תְּנוּ לִי	Hand me
עוֹד	A little
קְצָת	More

Dana Greitzer-Gotlieb is a rabbinical student at the Academy for Jewish Religion.

נרצה
Nirtzah

Never Again...
...Will I forget you

Rabbi Len Muroff

Excerpts from this reflection on a December 2023 Mission to Israel can be read before L'shana Ha'bah b'yerushalim.

There are so many thoughts cascading through my soul.

For one, I now feel closer to Israel and her people than any time since 1984. There is no "next year in Jerusalem" because my heart has been in Israel ever since October 7th. I will never forget my Israeli brothers and sisters, what they experienced that day, their resiliency since then, and their gratitude for each of us visiting in the middle of a war.

The Torah teaches us that we are to leave our mother and father and cleave to our spouse.[36] It is time for my deep bonds to Israel to be realized and respected. If I really mean that my "heart is in the east," then I must act accordingly.

---

[36] Gen. 2:24

The truth is, I have not thought about anything else since that horrific day, when we learned that murderous mobs had killed innocent people in Israel while they were just living their lives in their homes and communities.

I feel that it is finally time for me to be untethered from the Diaspora, open my heart, and to be connected more deeply to Israel, or more correctly and honestly, to make the cares and concerns of Israel just as much a focus and priority for me as that which I have for American political and cultural matters.

My trip to Israel in December 2023, was intense, meaningful, and gratifying. It was heavy but heartwarming. We carried home so much grief but also the knowledge that Israelis are both shuddering at what the future will be and perhaps more significantly rising to the occasion to create organizations and projects designed to supplement what the government just cannot get to because of the massive scale of the mobilization and the needs which have arisen.

I will never be the same person after this trip. What I saw at Kibbutz Kfar Aza was beyond the beyond. It was harder to absorb than my fifteen years doing hospice chaplaincy. The magnitude of the evil is beyond comprehension in America. It only begins to be real when you walk in the steps of the murderers and the victims. Our eyes saw a huge number of burned-out homes and innumerable bullet holes especially in the area where the young teens and twenties lived. There is no escaping the remnants of the murderous spree which until then had only been imagined. The pain and loss and emotional and spiritual impact on me/us were magnified by the banners hung from homes which included names and smiling pictures of the victims - attached to the front of their homes. They stated: *"this is where (insert name) was killed/brutally murdered or taken hostage."* It was unimaginably real, sad, and heart-breaking.

Then we were shown the destroyed homes of two of the three young men who were taken hostage then accidentally killed by the IDF just days before our visit to their now burned-out homes, which they could have helped rebuild. That caused my heart to break even more. There were no tears, just emotional paralysis. Words were insufficient to describe to each other what we were seeing and experiencing. We said "it is such a shame" / חבל but it is just not enough.

I saw the repair to the fence where the killers entered the kibbutz. I just shook my head, aghast as to the pain and fear that descended upon the members of each Kibbutz where attacks took place, shortly after the perimeters were breached.

It was an overwhelming experience to be where our people were slaughtered and treated so inhumanely. There was no ignoring the fact that we were walking where killers had shot people and ended lives and dreams. We walked the paths that had been home to our people and will be again.

We must have hope. We must learn how to simultaneously hold despair and hope. Both can and do exist at the same time.

Rabbi Len Muroff is rabbi at Temple Beth Ohr in La Mirada, CA.

Looking Forward, with Hope

Rabbi Debra Orenstein

Twice yearly, almost exactly six months apart, we sing out, "Next year in Jerusalem - *L'shanah Haba'ah B'yerushalayim.*" This rallying cry punctuates the Jewish calendar at the culmination of two major celebrations: Neilah, the last service of Yom Kippur and *Nirtzah*, the last portion of the Passover seder. Regardless of past slavery or sins, we eagerly anticipate improvement, rebuilding, and redemption.

For centuries, *L'shanah Haba'ah B'yerushalayim* expressed longing. Travel to and in the Land of Israel was rare and hazardous. Today, even in wartime, Jews simply take planes, trains, or automobiles to arrive in Jerusalem. Despite grief and danger, Jews are safer now than we were for most of Jewish history. We enjoy access to Jerusalem that our ancestors could only dream of.

From the time of Jeremiah (2,600+ years ago) until today, Jews have governed the land of Israel less than 7% of the time. In Israel and the Diaspora, our ancestors generally lived under foreign, unfriendly, rule. Insecure in their homes, they regularly endured inequality, expulsions, and violence.

Imagine Jews suffering blood libels during Passover (a popular season for them), yet still gathering, lifting the bread of affliction, and singing *Ha Lachma Anya*: "Now we are here. Next year in the land of Israel. This year, slaves. Next year, free."

How did they hold onto hope for a better year, next year – over decades, centuries, and most of the last two millennia?

One important answer is that hope itself has been a key ingredient in Jewish survival.

When Moses first approached the Israelites to announce that God would free them from slavery, they could not hear him, because of "shortened spirts and hard labor" (Ex. 6:8). Oppression takes its toll.

Initially, it was outside support that extended our ancestors' spirits and expanded their sense of possibility. Hope stemmed from the midwives' intervention, Moses' unwavering advocacy, the miracles of the plagues, and God's protection against the suffering that ensued. Then, God and Moses demanded that the Israelites take action to shape their own future: sacrifice a lamb, Pharaoh's consort animal; share the food; mark their doors with lamb's blood, thus branding themselves as rebels; pack and dress for travel;

set the communal calendar for a new month and a new life.

The Exodus narrative points to two essential elements of hope:

1. embracing support from powers beyond you, including Divine Power and
2. exercising your own power.

I call these the *Hope of Acceptance* and the *Hope of Agency*.

The Hope of Agency says: there is power within me to change things. The Hope of Acceptance says: there may be nothing I or we can change right now, but there are benign powers greater than we. Agency acts. Acceptance, well, *accepts* – its own limits and reliance on transcendent forces. The Hope of Agency works toward particular, cherished ends, while the Hope of Acceptance sustains a more global faith that a good future will unfold. For individuals and nations, both are needed. Depending on circumstances, each can be wise.

Judaism is a hopeful religion, despite calamities in our past and present. Hope was vital to our patriarchs, matriarchs, and prophets. Jewish liturgy, life cycle ritual, holidays, theology, and humor all reflect – and strengthen – great hope. Hope is necessary for *teshuvah* and *tikkun olam*; improvement and repair would not be attempted without *tikvah*, hope. Israel's anthem, *Hatikvah*, implicitly acknowledges that the House of Israel has, at times, felt, "our hope is lost,"[37] yet "our hope is still not lost."

Every Passover, we stoke our hope. Like those who experienced the Exodus, we gather to share a meal and the stories and journey of freedom. We remember the bitterness that we have overcome and recall the promise of redemption. Together, we sing that next year will be better.

Especially during hard times, it's important to realize that hope is essential for *making* next year better. Do whatever it takes to nurture your Agency and Acceptance, because hope is not just a good feeling about the future. It is the fuel we need to keep expanding our vision and collaborating to shape a better future.

Before the Israelites could know freedom, they had to have *hope* for freedom.

Before we can make peace, we need the *hope* that peace is possible.

I'll meet you out there in the future, in the Promised Land and the City of Peace.

Rabbi Debra Orenstein is the rabbi at Congregation B'nai Israel in Emerson, NJ.

---

[37] Ez. 37:11

Forward Together

Julie Brandon

The sea calls to me
To stand and wait
For the miracle to happen
For the song that follows
Shall we wade into the water
Buoyed up by faith and trust
Grab my hand
We'll cross together
Never to forget the bondage
For if we do, how can we help others break free
Hold my hand and take that first step
As we reach freedom together

Julie Brandon is a poet, playwright and lyricist with an emphasis on Jewish liturgical music.

ספירת העמר
Counting the Omer

סְפִירָה / Sefirah: The Counting[38]
Rabbi Joseph H. Prouser

לְשֵׁם יְחוּד הַקָּטוּפִים
וּמִשְׁפְּחוֹתֵיהֶם, בְּשֵׁם כָּל
יִשְׂרָאֵל.

In the cause of reuniting the hostages with their families, in the name of all Israel.

הִנְנִי מוּכָן וּמְזֻמָּן לְקַיֵּם
מִצְוַת עֲשֵׂה שֶׁל סְפִירָה,
כַּכָּתוּב:

I am about to fulfill the Mitzvah of counting, as it is written: This is what the Lord says,

כֹּה אָמַר יְיָ מִנְעִי קוֹלֵךְ
מִבֶּכִי וְעֵינַיִךְ מִדִּמְעָה
כִּי יֵשׁ שָׂכָר לִפְעֻלָּתֵךְ נְאֻם־
יְיָ וְשָׁבוּ מֵאֶרֶץ אוֹיֵב:
וְיֵשׁ־תִּקְוָה לְאַחֲרִיתֵךְ
נְאֻם־יְיָ וְשָׁבוּ בָנִים
לִגְבוּלָם:

"Restrain your voice from weeping and your eyes from tears, for your work will be rewarded," declares the Lord. "They will return from the land of the enemy. So there is hope for your future," declares the Lord. "Your children shall return to their country."[39]

וְכַכָּתוּב: וּפְדוּיֵי יְיָ יְשׁוּבוּן
וּבָאוּ צִיּוֹן בְּרִנָּה וְשִׂמְחַת
עוֹלָם עַל־רֹאשָׁם שָׂשׂוֹן
וְשִׂמְחָה יַשִּׂיגוּן נָסוּ יָגוֹן
וַאֲנָחָה:

And as it is written: "Those redeemed by the Lord will enter Zion with singing, and everlasting joy will crown their heads. Gladness and joy will overtake them, and sighing will cease."[40]

---

[38] Prepared in advance for Seder night 2024, it is our fervent prayer that this sad ritual of counting the days that Israeli men, women, elders, and infants have been held hostage in Gaza will -- with their release -- be rendered unnecessary and outdated long before Pesach arrives.

[39] Jeremiah 31:16-17

[40] Isaiah 51:11

בָּרוּךְ יְיָ אֲשֶׁר לֹא הִשְׁבִּית
לְךָ גֹּאֵל הַיּוֹם:

(בְּלֵיל סֵדֶר רִאשׁוֹן) הַיּוֹם
יוֹם מֵאָה תִּשְׁעִים וְתֵשַׁע.

(בְּלֵיל סֵדֶר שֵׁנִי) הַיּוֹם
מָאתַיִם יוֹם.

הָרַחֲמָן הוּא יַחֲזִיר לָנוּ
אַחֵינוּ כֹּל בֵּית יִשְׂרָאֵל
הַנְּתוּנִים בְּצָרָה וּבַשִּׁבְיָה,
בִּמְהֵרָה בְיָמֵינוּ אָמֵן סֶלָה.

Blessed are You, Who
has not withheld
redemption this day![41]

[At the first Seder:]
**Today is 199 days of
captivity.**

[At the second Seder:]
**Today is 200 days of
captivity.**

May a merciful God
return to us all our
brethren among the
House of Israel
who are in distress or
held in captivity.
Speedily. Today. Amen.
Selah.

---

[41] Ruth 4:14

141

שירים
Songs and Poems

For Chad Gadya

Rabbi Robert Scheinberg, PhD

In his commentary to the Haggadah, the eminent
Israeli Talmud scholar Rabbi Adin Steinsaltz
imagines a child trying to make sense of Chad
Gadya, the unusual song with which we
conclude the Seder. He suggests: A child might
read this song as a poem about vengeance and
justice. An apparently innocent goat who is eaten
by a cat, and then a dog bites the cat. Steinsaltz's
hypothetical child assumes this dog is a noble,
justice-loving animal who, having witnessed the
cruel unprovoked attack against the blameless
goat, seeks to punish the cat for this nefarious
deed.

Next, the stick beats the dog -- so presumably, the
stick is an ally of the cat. The child begins to sort
the characters in this story into two teams: the
evil Team Cat, who cause the suffering of the
innocent and perpetrate reprisals upon those
who challenge their right to do so, and the noble
Team Dog, who empathize with the suffering of
the innocent goat and seek to punish those who
victimized it.

The fire burns the stick - so the fire is on Team
Dog. The water that extinguishes the fire is on
Team Cat. The ox that drinks the water is on the
noble Team Dog, and the *shochet* is on the evil
Team Cat. The Angel of Death is on the noble
Team Dog … which means that the Holy Blessed

One is on the evil Team Cat, defending those who would cause harm to the innocent. At this point, the child is deeply troubled. How can God be on the side of the cat that ate the goat?!

For Rabbi Steinsaltz, the answer to this conundrum is clear: Chad Gadya could not possibly be a story about vengeance. The dog doesn't bite the cat out of allegiance to the goat; rather, biting cats is simply part of the dog's nature. There is no Team Dog or Team Cat; there are just various animals, objects, and individuals that act violently because of their own short-sighted motivations. The enemy of my enemy is not my friend.

And yet it's not just children who are inclined to see the world with black-and-white moral clarity in which some acts of violence are absolutely noble and other acts of violence are absolutely evil. Chad Gadya is fated to continue until someone breaks the cycle.

Chad Gadya is a prominent trope in Israeli poetry about war and violence.

Yehuda Amichai prayed[42] that his son and his neighbor's son wouldn't get caught in the wheels of the fearsome Chad Gadya machine. Chava Alberstein sang[43] of the futility of Chad Gadya's cycle of attackers being attacked and pursuers being pursued. And Levin Kipnis imagined[44] the

---

"רועה ערבי מחפש גדי" (יהודה עמיחי, 1987) [42]

"חד גדיא" (חוה אלברשטיין, 1989) [43]

"חד גדיא" (לוין קיפניס, 1942) [44]

beautiful community that could be created if these Chad Gadya characters managed to get along.

Religious poems don't exist to provide us with specific policy guidelines, to tell us exactly how to protect ourselves from the predators who seek to do us harm. Rather, poems plant values within us: If you are too fixated on revenge, you end up creating a topsy-turvy world in which God ends up on the wrong side.

Somehow, we'll have to learn to turn the page from Chad Gadya-style violence, even though the Haggadah's next page is blank. We'll have to write it together.

Rabbi Robert Scheinberg is rabbi at United Synagogue of Hoboken. He is also Interim Rabbi-in-Residence at the Academy for Jewish Religion.

קול דודי ,כל דודי
The voice of my beloved
All of my beloved
Rabbi Hanna Yerushalmi

Awake, north wind,
Come, south wind,
Find my beloved one
And bring him back
From this long captivity.

Tell me, where are you?
How have you passed the hours?
Are there gray doves nearby
keeping you company
With their rolling coos.

How I miss sitting with you
Peacefully in the cool shade.
Your left arm under my head,
Your right arm embracing me,
A banner of love around us.

Awake, north wind,
Come, south wind,
Search deep in the lower valley
And explore the crevices of the wide plain
Until my love appears and comes home.

The blossoms emerge in the land,
The winter is past and the rains are over,
But you are still missing for so long.
I linger in the garden, and whisper,
Hurry back to me, my beloved.

I wait and wait for the day of your release
When you will again be a seal upon my heart
When I can cry out to the mountains:
Kol Dodi, I hear the voice of my beloved!
Kol Dodi, I embrace all of you, my beloved!

Rabbi Hanna Yerushalmi is a licensed professional counselor and is a writer, teacher, and motivational group leader.

Ana Eili – To You I Call

Max Halperin

אָנָּא אֵלִי, אֵלֶיךָ אֶקְרָא

שֶׁהֲמַת הַשִּׂנְאָה הַשּׁוֹרֶרֶת בְּעֵינֵי אָדָם בְּפִיו וּבְיָדָיו.

תְּחַבְּלָהּ בְּאַהֲבָה

שַׁבְּרָהּ בְּבִינָה

רַטְּשָׁהּ בִּגְשִׁירָה

קַטְּלָהּ בִּדְבִיקָה

צַמְּתָהּ בְּהַכָּרָה

פַּגְּרָהּ בּוֹעֵידָה

עַקְּרָהּ בְּזָכְיָה

סַפֵּהּ בְּחֹבָה

נַדֵּהּ בְּטוֹבָה

מַחֲקָהּ בִּידִיעָה

לַהֲטָהּ בִּכְלִילָה

כַּלֵּהּ בִּלְמִידָה

יַסְּרָהּ בִּמְחִילָה

טַרְפָהּ בְּנֶחָמָה

חַסְּלָהּ בְּסְלִיחָה

זַעֲרָהּ בְּעֶזְרָה

וַתְּרָהּ בִּפְגִישָׁה

הַמֵּמָהּ בִּצְדָקָה

דַּכֵּהּ בִּקְרִיבָה

גַּדְּעָהּ בִּרְחִימָה

בַּטְּלָהּ בִּשְׁמִיעָה

אַבְּדָהּ בְּתִקְוָה

מְבֹרָךְ אַבְרָהָם וְשָׂרָה, הַבָּא יוֹם שֶׁלֹּא נִצְטָרֵךְ לְהַכּוֹת וְלִרְדֹּף שׂוֹנְאֵינוּ

וְכָל בְּנֵי הָאָדָם בְּיַחַד יִסְעֲדוּ לְבָם.

מְבֹרָךְ יִצְחָק וְרִבְקָה, שִׂים עֹשֶׂק וְשִׂטְנָה מֵאַחֲרֵנוּ וְהַרְאֵנוּ אֶת הַמָּקוֹם

שֶׁהָרְחַבְתָּ לְכֻלָּנוּ.

מְבֹרָךְ יַעֲקֹב וְלֵאָה וְרָחֵל, קָרֵב אֵלֵנוּ עֵת שֶׁנּוּכַל לְחַבֵּק אֶת אֹיְבֵינוּ וְשֶׁנֵּלֵךְ

לְדַרְכֵּנוּ בְּשָׁלוֹם.

כַּכָּתוּב עַל יַד נְבִיאֶךָ 'וְכִתְּתוּ חַרְבוֹתָם לְאִתִּים וַחֲנִיתוֹתֵיהֶם לְמַזְמֵרוֹת לֹא

יִשָּׂא גוֹי אֶל גּוֹי חֶרֶב וְלֹא יִלְמְדוּ עוֹד מִלְחָמָה'.

כֵּן יְהִי רָצוֹן כֵּן יְהִי רָצוֹן כֵּן יְהִי רָצוֹן

אָמֵן אָמֵן אָמֵן סֶלָה

Please my God, to You I call
That You will bring out the death of the hatred
that festers in the eyes of humankind, in its
mouths and in its hands.
Wound it with love
Shatter it with understanding
Dismember it with bridging
Slaughter it with clinging
Lessen it with recognition
Cadaver it with coupling
Uproot it with merit
End it with affection
Expel it with goodness
Erase it with knowledge
Incinerate it with inclusion
Finish it with learning
Torment it with pardon
Devour it with comfort
Complete it with forgiveness
Shrink it with aid
Renounce it with meeting
Stun it with righteousness
Disadvantage it with closeness
Sever it with mercy
Abolish it with listening
Exterminate it with hope

You who blessed Avraham and Sarah, bring the
day when we will no longer need to wound and
pursue our adversaries, and all of humankind
can together nourish their souls.

You who blessed Yitzchak and Rivkah, put
bickering and animosity behind us, and show us
the place with enough space for all of us.

You who blessed Yaakov, Leah and Rachel, bring us closer to the time that we can embrace our enemies, and we can go on our paths in peace.

As is written by the hand of Your prophet, "And they shall beat their swords into plowshares And their spears into pruning hooks. Nation shall not take up sword against nation; they shall never again know war."

So may it be willed, so may it be willed, so may it be willed. Amen amen amen, full stop.

Max Halperin is a rabbinical student and poet.

Karev Yom
Rachel Braun

The words framed by the ombré shading pattern are *karev yom asher hu lo yom ve'lo layla* ("Draw near a day that is neither day nor night"). They come from a piyyut by Yannai, a payyetan, liturgical poet, writing in 7th century Israel. His poem, Vayehi beHatzi haLayla ("It happened at midnight", from Exodus 12:29), is included in the Passover haggadah for the first seder. An alphabetical acrostic, the piyyut lists miracles that occurred at midnight on Passover, the timing of the Exodus of the Israelites from Egypt. Drawing on rabbinic imagination, these events include Abraham's mustering of troops to save his nephew Lot, Jacob's wrestling with the angel, Daniel's interpretation of Nebuchadnezzar's dream, and more. The embroidered phrase begins with the Hebrew letter kuf, falling late in the poem when the payyetan's attention turns to anticipation of future redemption. It refers to the Messianic vision of Zekhariah 14:7: "There shall be a continuous day— only the Lord knows when—of neither day nor night, and there shall be light at eventide". Initially, I was attracted to this verse simply musically, remembering a cheerful tune celebrating the coming of the Messiah. Later, I learned a more contemplative melody. Which melody reveals the correct interpretation? Cheerful and toe-tapping, or contemplative and swaying? Day or night? It is hard to characterize the Messianic experience, a vast unknown, one that feels far removed from our current experience. In crafting the design, I sought elements that conveyed my interpretation of the words. I drew letters that had an austere, imposing stance, to reflect the boldness of Yannai's vision of the special midnight intimacy of God with the people Israel. The color palette ranged from light blue to dark navy and back again, representing the fluidity of day and night in Zekhariah's imagination of the Messianic age. I suppose that the embroidery resolves my musical dilemma in favor of the second, more serious melody, as the severity of the long rectangle evokes the challenge of waiting for the Messianic age.

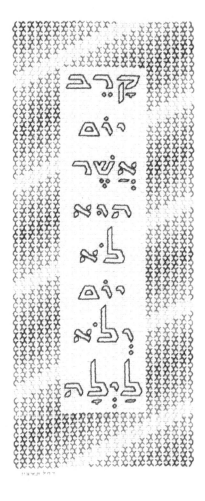

Rachel Braun, "Karev Yom"

Made in the USA
Las Vegas, NV
11 April 2024